Physical Education in the early years

The early years are dynamic times for children as they pass through a mainly sensory motor stage, into a period where they will still need an action-based and enjoyable curriculum in order to capture their interest. Finally, they will move into a phase where they will develop all the motor skills and patterns which they will need in order to sustain the rigours of normal life.

This book begins with an overview of the first months of a child's life, with an indication of the major movement milestones which all children should reach before they enter the pre-school phase. The rest of the book gives information about developing children's physical skills in dance, games and gymnastics throughout the pre-school and infant school phase. It also addresses many of the contemporary issues surrounding the delivery of the PE curriculum in schools including the assessment of pupil's performance.

This book will help students, teachers and curriculum leaders deliver a sound PE education to children aged 3–7, and will also prove useful to all those involved in early years education.

Pauline Wetton is currently a Lecturer in Education and Assistant Director of Sport at the University of Durham.

Teaching and Learning in the First Three Years of School

Series Editor *Joy Palmer*

This innovatory and up-to-date series is concerned specifically with curriculum practice in the first three years of school. Each book includes guidance on:

- subject content
- planning and organisation
- assessment and record-keeping
- in-service training

This practical advice is placed in the context of the National Curriculum and the latest theoretical work on how children learn at this age and what experiences they bring to their early years in the classroom.

Other books in the series:

Physical Education in the early years

Pauline Wetton

London and New York

First published 1997
by Routledge
11 New Fetter Lane, London EC4P 4EE

Simultaneously published in the USA and Canada
by Routledge
29 West 35th Street, New York, NY 10001

Typeset in Palatino by
Ponting–Green Publishing Services, Chesham,
Buckinghamshire
Printed and bound in Great Britain by
Mackays of Chatham PLC, Chatham, Kent

British Library Cataloguing in Publication Data
A catalogue record for this book is available from the
British Library

Library of Congress Cataloguing in Publication Data
Wetton, Pauline
    Physical education in the early years / Pauline Wetton.
        p.   cm. – (Teaching and learning in the first three
years at school)
    Includes bibliographical references (p.   ).
    1. Physical education for children–Study and teaching
(Early childhood)–Great Britain.   2. Physical education
for children–Great Britain–Curricula–Planning
I. Title.   II. Series: Teaching and learning in the first
three years of school.
GV443.W445   1996
372.86–dc21   96–52979

ISBN   0–415–13529–x

Contents

Series editor's preface

Each book in this series focuses on a specific curriculum area. The series relates relevant learning theory or a rationale for early years learning to the practical development and implementation of subject-based topics and classroom activities at the infant level (i.e., Reception, Year 1, Year 2). It seems that the majority of existing books on primary education and the primary curriculum focus on pupils aged 7–11 years. It is hoped that this series presents a refreshing and much needed change in that it specifically addresses the first three years in school.

Each volume is intended to be an up-to-date, judicious mix of theory and practical classroom application, offering a wealth of background information, ideas and advice to all concerned with planning, implementing, monitoring and evaluating teaching and learning in the first three years in school. Theoretical perspectives are presented in a lively and interesting way, drawing upon recent classroom research findings wherever possible. Case studies and activities from a range of classrooms and schools illuminate many of the substantial issues related to the subject area in question.

Readers will find a similar pattern of contents in all the books in the series. Each discusses the early learning environment, transition from home- to school-based learning, and addresses the key questions of what this means for the early years teacher and the curriculum. Such discussion inevitably incorporates ideas on the knowledge which young children may have of subjects and an overview of the subject matter itself which is under scrutiny. As the thrust of the series is towards young children learning subjects, albeit in a holistic way, no doubt readers will wish to consider what is an appropriate content or rationale for the subject in the early years. Having considered young children as learners, what they are bringing into school in terms of prior knowledge, the teacher's task and the subject matter itself, each book then turns its attention to appropriate methods of planning, organising, implementing and evaluating teaching and learning activities. Crucial matters such as assessment, evaluation and record-keeping are dealt with in their own right, and are also referred to and discussed in ongoing examples of good practice. Each book concludes with useful suggestions for further staffroom discussion/INSET activities and advice on resources.

As a whole, the series aims to be inspirational and forward-looking. As all readers know so well, the National Curriculum is not 'written in concrete'. Education is a dynamic process. While taking due account of the essential National Curriculum framework, authors go far beyond the level of description of rigid content guidelines to highlight *principles* for teaching and learning. Furthermore, they incorporate two key messages which surely underpin successful, reflective education, namely 'vision' and 'enthusiasm'. It is hoped that students and teachers will be inspired and assisted in their task of implementing successful and progressive plans which help young learners to make sense of their world and the key areas of knowledge within it.

Joy A. Palmer

Preface

Most books written on physical education for children in the 3–7 years age group have been published in response to the requests of teachers and students who felt that they needed prescriptive texts to enable them to provide children with an action-packed programme.

Such prescriptive tests have recently included information which has guided teachers through the implementation of the National Curriculum, both pre- and post-Dearing. The National Curriculum has acted as a catalyst in most schools and has allowed teachers to redefine each subject as it has been reintroduced within the framework of the post-Dearing curriculum. Early years educators have worked hard in producing effective programmes for the core curriculum subjects and have been successful in their implementation. Unfortunately a similar treatment has not always been possible for the subject called Physical Education.

My concern in writing this book is that the quality of early years education in Great Britain, which used to be admired internationally, is gradually being eroded. The call for universal pre-school education for instance, which is intended to increase the number of places available to our youngest children, will result in a poorer quality of educational provision unless more money is released into the system to provide more teachers and more resources. I have increasing concerns about the prescriptive approach to PE in infant schools, which has arisen from the paucity of curriculum time which is apportioned to it by those who train those students who eventually teach classes in infant schools. Fewer and fewer teachers are trained to know how children learn through involvement in Physical Education activities and unless the balance is redressed, we will be guilty of losing what was such an important facet of early years education. Recent research data, conducted by the Principles into Practice Research Group (Blenkin and Yue 1995), whose work focuses on the professional development of practitioners working with children under 8, demonstrated that head teachers working in every type of setting ranked the knowledge of child development as the most important factor in the professional development of teachers. It is clear that these head teachers, of both state and private schools, whilst seeing curriculum content as important, still view the knowledge about young children's development as the real basis of appropriate provision and practice. Ironically, child development no longer holds a central place in the training of early years teachers. This facet of teacher training has been squeezed out by the requirement for student teachers to study National Curriculum subjects and the assessment of pupils' performances.

I consider therefore that it is timely to reassess the programmes which are being produced for children in this age group and to examine what I consider to be 'good practice' in relation to effective learning in Physical Education activities and to the understanding of child development which is crucial if children are to develop competence in physical skill acquisition.

Introduction

This book is about the physical development of young children. Its key theme is that if physical development is to take place, then a dialogue should exist between the learner and the adult. Although this dialogue will be evident in several forms, its principal focus will always be on knowledgeable and experienced adults passing on information to the less knowledgeable and less experienced children. The book also examines the notion that since children are bio-cultural individuals who have become what they are by being nurtured and through their genetic inheritance, it is important that adults communicate to them their essential differences and provide them with differentiated activities so that they can all succeed.

In practical terms, the book emphasises the importance of continuous visual observation, assessment and evaluation of children's performances in which adults must become involved if all normal children are to acquire the motor skills and motor patterns which they will need to learn before they are 7. Some suggestions for learning goals are offered in each chapter and some guidelines on the physical performance levels which children should be able to achieve at the end of each age phase are set out. These practical guidelines are linked to contemporary issues currently affecting the wider debate concerning the teaching of Physical Education, e.g., *Sport: Raising the Game* (Department of National Heritage 1995); the importance of an active lifestyle; the 4-year-old in school; and the importance of offering a well-balanced and developmental curriculum.

In detail, the book begins with an examination of the years before school, when children are passing through the sensori-motor phase. The physical development which occurs at this stage is linked to the 'moving milestones' which children achieve before they enter the pre-school phase. All this activity is discussed in order to highlight the continuity which should exist across the whole age phase 0–7 years when examining the manner in which physical skills and motor patterns are acquired. The pre-school phase is then separated into two chapters, one which examines the essential nature of the nursery school setting and the other, the 4-year-old in school. Here, reference is made to current research which shows the decline in activity programmes, and information on good practice is offered by way of compensation. Other contributory factors which are gradually affecting the British population, e.g. obesity and the imbalance between nutrition and energy expenditure, are examined.

The impact of the National Curriculum in relation to the teaching of Physical Education is highlighted throughout the discussions on children's developing skills. The National Curriculum in relation to Physical Education would appear to have been flexibly structured to allow teachers to deliver a sound curriculum to their children. Nevertheless, the point is made that the impact of delivering the core curriculum, and the introduction of so many foundation subjects, seems to have both exhausted the teaching force and crowded the timetable. Consequently, a neglect of the essential right of children to be active together, coupled with a decline in teacher knowledge about how children acquire transferable gross motor and fine motor bodily skills, is seen as a regrettable result of current educational pressure.

There are three separate chapters which explore each of the Programmes of Study in the National Curriculum in Physical Education. Material is offered which has been gathered from various schools to create a suggested Programme of Study for teachers to use in delivering the curriculum. Each chapter is different in style because of the essential differences in the manner in which the three areas are learned. For example, the gymnastic activities curriculum is seen as a two-year programme where differentiation is offered by giving children tasks which can be solved by outcome, whereas the games programme is structured across a developmental continuum where children are offered new strategies for learning as they become ready to acquire them. In the games curriculum, activities are differentiated by task, whilst the chapter on dance discusses the notion of dance and all the variations which exist within the genre. The impossibility of structuring a programme which can offer so many different methods of delivery and so many stimuli to assist children's aesthetic development is discussed within the chapter, and sample lessons are suggested. Whilst all the chapters have a very strong practical base, consideration is given to a number of important issues related to the physical activities offered. These include a full discussion of special needs, with special emphasis on the reasons why a growing number of children are developing motor problems, as well as an examination of those factors which are leading more children to spend more time indoors on sedentary rather than physically driven activities.

The last chapter is devoted totally to the planning and assessment of a school Physical Education curriculum. Here, guidelines are offered for whole school planning, together with some suggestions for the role of the curriculum leader, INSET activities and strategies. Examples of how to record children's performances at the end of the Key Stage are illustrated by three case studies.

Chapter 1

How do young children learn to move?
The parental role

From the moment that their children are born most parents are intensely interested in the 'moving milestone events' in their children's lives. The first movements which babies make – considered to be reflexive in nature – are eagerly anticipated, so that the first proper smile is hailed as an indicator that, at last, their child can make a responsive physical movement. From that moment on, it seems that babies begin to learn the essential pre-requisites for learning to move as both their sight develops and their limb movements become more co-ordinated.

The sight of newborn babies is limited to a small area of about 22–26cms from their eyes. Anything which is nearer or further away is blurred. At first then, they focus on faces and objects which are within this sight range. As their range of vision increases, however, they begin to practice following with their eyes as the need for following objects and faces in their environment grows. Thus, in the first few weeks of life, babies practise this eye co-ordination for most of their waking life. At the same time, too, they begin to lose the foetal positioning of their limbs, and the reflex action of grasping anything which is placed in their hands develops into an ability to move their arms. Babies soon become capable of watching their own hands as they cross their faces. They also begin to watch familiar faces which come into and out of their limited visionary pathways. The beginning of visual perception is being established as babies start the first stage on the pathway of motor skill learning, that of practice and experience.

The phenomenon of motor learning is internal and takes place within the central nervous system. Since it cannot be observed directly, all we can do is to observe the performance of infants and draw an inference about the learning which seems to be taking place. The initial stages of any new skill appear to be learned in a step-by-step manner so, at first, young learners seem to be awkward and disorganised in their attempts. However, the more they practise the more their co-ordination improves. Consequently, if we observe improvement in performance it is possible to suggest that learning is taking place, although the learner must then be observed to be able to repeat the skill on many occasions before it is reasonable to say that the learner has acquired or learned the particular motor skill.

Fitts and Posner (1967) have offered a clear model of the motor skill learning process. They have described three stages in motor learning – the cognitive, the associative and the autonomous phases. However, this model is perhaps easier to apply when children are in the more mature stages of infant motor skill learning. A more appropriate model for babies and toddlers is a simplistic processing model where the learner begins the business of acquiring a skill through the presence of some external trigger mechanism which invites a response from the learner. Here, the baby receives some kind of sensation from the environment, e.g., the face of a sibling which comes into focus. As the baby perceives and recognises the shape and form of the face, the baby reaches to touch it. At this stage, then, the sequence is environmental trigger, perception by the baby, and finally motor response. As this happens, and particularly as the processing model becomes more sophisticated, babies appear to store the information they receive. However, they do need stimulation and a conducive environment if they are to practise and learn those movements which will enable them to take a step forwards towards the next moving milestone. It is equally important, too, that parents need to be informed about the stages which babies go through in the normal processes of physical development, motor skill learning and acquisition. At the same time, they also need to be keen observers of the developing motor capacities of infants.

It is an interesting fact that many parents contribute to the emerging physical and motor development capability of their children almost without realising that they are doing so. For example, placing a mobile over a cot to produce movement and shape patterns is an excellent stimulus for visual perception as babies begin to track the movement with their eyes. This eye tracking movement eventually leads to babies starting to turn their heads and lift their chins, but how many parents know that this is happening? Placing and securing a soft toy at the side of a cot or pram – another popular parental strategy – encourages babies to reach out and touch with their hands, which is another stage in motor development. Here, partial turning of the head and body follows this early reaching which, in turn, strengthens the muscles of the body ready for later and more complex movement learning. Using a baby's visual perception to encourage movement is highly important, as is the use of auditory stimulus which also plays a valuable part in early movement practice and movement learning. All babies enjoy the action of being rocked, particularly if an adult sings to them at the same time. This stimulus of rhythmic movement accompanied by rhythmic sound was frequently a commonplace activity as parents sang lullabies to their offspring. As an early introduction to rhythm such an activity is ideal, especially for laying the foundations for dance activities in early childhood. Another auditory stimulus which can help babies practise movement is through the suspension of toys and shapes containing bells or other sound-producing objects over the place where they are lying. If these are suspended close enough for babies to reach out and touch, they will soon reach a stage when they can cause the objects to move and thus more movement practice will ensue. If babies wiggle their hands and wave their arms with delight at the sounds which are made, then so much the better!

Another auditory practice which can assist babies' fine motor skill learning is to use the stimulus of a rattle. Babies like to make noises with objects. Initially, they are quite happy to grasp a rattle and shake it or guide it towards their mouth to chew it, but eventually they begin to sense that they can make the movement which results in sound. All these activities give babies the opportunity to practise movement co-ordination skills and to focus their eyes and hands on both static and moving objects, both of which are important for later games playing. Also at this stage, babies become aware that toys and faces can go out of their sight range, so that a game like 'Peep!' can be introduced to develop perceptual awareness, as well as providing huge social enjoyment for the players playing it! Gradually, through stretching to reach for objects and through the early flexing and stretching of limbs whilst lying in a supine position, babies develop strength in the muscles of their backs. They begin to kick their legs extensively and wave their arms vigorously when they are placed in a supine position on different surfaces. They also begin to lift up their heads and chests to see their world when they are lying in a prone position.

Initially babies are carried and supported by adults as they are transported from place to place but, as they become stronger, they can begin to sit on an adult's knee with support. Many adults often enjoy sharing singing rhymes with babies as they support them in this position. Most of these rhymes have accompanying actions which give babies an experience of keeping themselves upright whilst the adult holds their hands. Actions can also give babies a sensation of the early feeling of balancing their bodies in an upright position. All these changes of position increase babies' postural control, an important developmental step in the processes of acquiring motor control of the spine and movement development.

The first significant moving milestone, then, is the day when babies can be observed to turn from the supine position to the prone position; eventually they will be able to roll over from one position to the other with ease. This is a 'performance' which is easily observed and which can be assessed as a gross motor skill which has been acquired. Nobody can fail to be impressed either with the performance of babies who switch from upright sitting to crawling, and then back to sitting again. They learn this complicated manoeuvre in a short time in their lifespan. It would seem that they have been gradually getting strong enough to hold a sitting posture and have practised moving from position to position until they have mastered the process.This is another example of the processing model of movement learning described earlier.

The skills which are now being learned, however, are much more complex. It cannot be claimed with certainty that babies know or understand the purpose of the task nor could it be argued that there has been a high level of cognition at work in their actions. What does seem likely is that there is evidence, yet again, of an evironmental trigger at work which has caused them to move. It may be the case that babies know the relevance of the task and that they have developed some semblance of the appropriate body transference skills needed to complete it. If this is so, then, even at this stage, there is probably some crude evaluation taking place of what is happening to them, but it could not be classed as a sophisticated analysis in movement learning model terms. A simple scenario might be that babies fall backwards many times in their search for sitting stature stability. On occasions, they will also have fallen sideways before learning to put their hands at the sides of their bodies. Only when they have learned from these experiences will they then attempt to put their weight on their hands to support themselves in the initial stages of moving on to their knees and beginning to crawl.

After this first milestone, subsequent milestones are reached comparatively quickly. These can be categorised as the day when babies move by crawling on their hands and knees or lurch along on their bottoms, the day when they start to pull themselves up and begin to stand on their feet whilst holding on to furniture, the day when they climb up the stairs, the day when they have acquired enough strength to stand unaided and finally the day when they take their first step. How many parents stop and think 'How did they learn to do that?'

The physical milestones which all parents can observe have been formally recorded by Dr Mary Sheridan, who, after reviewing some of the earlier development scales produced by Gesell, Buhler, Ilingworth and Griffiths, produced the Stycar Schedules (1969) which she calls 'stepping stones' in children's development. Her schedules are based on observations of babies and toddlers in clinics, nurseries, schools and hospitals. One of the four main sections in these schedules is that which is related to posture and large movements of the body. The order in which movement and physical skills emerge in her stepping stone sequences is exactly the order in which most parents will have observed them. It would seem to be such a common occurrence that it is not surprising parents do not concern themselves with this phenomenon (except to revel and rejoice as each stage is reached!) nor wonder how the child learned these skills. The study of this phenomenon, however, contributes to our understanding of human variation, something which is vitally important. Children do not, of course, reach these stepping stones of movement achievement at the same time, for whilst the growth of children's bodies is a very regular and organised process – a product of the continuous and complex interaction of both heredity and environment – it does not follow that they will grow at the same rate or at an even rate. The genetic or hereditary factor is very important in both children's growth process and in children's eventual size. Physique, heredity and environment play a definite part in the time and onset of both upright posture and walking.

Once children can walk, their waking life is usually concerned with gross motor activity and it goes without saying that a happy toddler is an active toddler! Now they can go anywhere and are only limited by the boundaries set by others. Their locomotor patterns will develop in a normative sequence if they have access to a suitable and safe place to be involved in movement play. If children are given the opportunity, it is certain that they will acquire the mature walking pattern and all the possible walking pattern variations, by practising them for themselves. They are also capable of developing a series of eye–hand co-ordination skills, although these will only be acquired with the intervention of an older person who can give instructions and encouragement. Children will walk and eventually toddle quickly to greet a known sibling, or to chase a dog, and will climb up on to furniture, will bounce on beds, will climb the stairs in the normal course of daily living, but they will not learn how to catch, bat or kick a ball unless a more experienced person assists them.

Parents, however, are busy people. If they want to help their children, then they have to incorporate their children's movement learning into their own daily work plans. They may not be concerned about how their children are learning to move or how they are acquiring physical skills; indeed, for many parents there is an almost automatic assumption that their children acquire them through normal processes of development. The development and refinement of skilful performance in a variety of activities, however, is one of the major tasks of childhood, and should not be taken for granted. It is heartening to note, therefore, the increasing number of parents who recognise this fact. Nowadays, for instance, a large proportion of parents sense the need to ensure that their children are confident in water, whilst others are beginning to use the network of Tumble Tots clubs which provide gymnastic-type activities for toddlers. Significantly, there is much more parental use of the many toddler groups which are located in sports centres and activity centres which are being created in family rooms attached to public houses. Children can buy one hour of active play in these locations which have varied names such as 'Wacky Warehouse', 'Charlie Chalk', or 'Deep Sea Den'. It is interesting to hear the various reasons given for involving children in these activities. For example, one parent told me that although he had observed that his 2-year-old child was linguistically advanced for his age, the child did not seem to be competent in various physical situations, and so the parent felt that his son needed some help in a supportive physical play environment. Another parent reported that she was anxious about her 2-year-old daughter who, although very active in the home situation, was thought to need the more challenging environment of the Tumble Tots club to develop her physical skills.

There are, of course, other settings where parents who sense the need for their children to be more active can send their children to play – the garden, for instance. However, many children do not live in such protective settings and may find themselves spending a considerable part of their early lives on the streets. Although many people would consider the street to be a rather dangerous place for youngsters nowadays, it is a far better place for children to learn the essential gross motor and locomotor movement skills effectively than to be cloistered in the home with little or no incentive to become involved in robust physical play at all.

However, it would seem that more and more parents do have a growing awareness of the need for their children to be involved in physical play and many are becoming competent in the formative assessment of their own children's special physical needs. Malina and Bouchard (1991) suggest that a child's physical performance characteristics are related in part to his/her growth, maturation and development. They state that growth and maturation are essentially biological processes, whilst the concept of development has a broader range, involving behavioural domains. Physical performance, they suggest, includes both these biological and behavioural domains, and children should therefore be classified as bio-cultural or bio-social individuals. If this is so, and children are indeed bio-social or bio-cultural individuals, then the home and those who control the boundaries and activities in the home environment are very influential in determining what children will learn and how they will learn it before they enter the school system.

Eventually, when 3-year-old children come to pre-school, even though they are all of the same chronological age, they will be observed to be of different heights, weights and body shapes relative to each other, and educators should be aware of these variations.

Chapter 2

Physical Education in pre-school environments

It is reasonable to assume (Malina and Bouchard 1991, Corbin 1973, Dennis 1940) that infants arriving from the womb are already shaped by their genetic inheritance and are capable of a number of motor responses which are, it is believed, of a reflex nature. Theorists, however, are divided about the next stage in children's motor learning. There are those who present the general hypothesis that children's ability to learn physical skills is controlled initially by biological growth, and who believe that children's nerve circuits unfold inevitably, requiring no specific intervention (Gesell 1928, Dennis and Dennis 1940, McGraw 1945, Bower 1966), whilst there are others who believe that children depend on the environment and adult intervention if they are to acquire physical skill at the optimum time (Espenschade and Eckert 1967, Cratty 1973, Malina and Bouchard 1991, Gallahue 1995). Both groups would agree, however, with the general hypothesis that training children to acquire physical tasks before their bodies are biologically able to assimilate them is untenable. They almost certainly believe that genetic inheritance and speed of biological maturation does tend to modify or supplant the results of training.

It is therefore crucially important that those concerned with the education of children become keen observers and are especially aware of when children are biologically ready to acquire a skill. Having ascertained this, educators must then ensure that the correct and most suitable provision is offered to enable children to acquire that skill. In other words, children should be given every opportunity to practise the skill, so that not only will the educator be able to make a formative assessment, but will be ready to interact at the optimum time to enable children to refine it. It would seem reasonable to assume that if children are to learn to move and to acquire physical skill then educators must recognise the biological, the behavioural and the social domain in which the child is nurtured. Generally, those who teach in pre-school environments are well aware of the nature and complexity of the children who enter their establishments each year. For the most part, they are also aware of the different home cultures in which the children have been nurtured. They are also fully cognisant of the need to provide a safe and stable atmosphere in the pre-school so that, initially, routines become commonplace and children can feel secure enough to choose to play with the physical objects in the indoor and outdoor environment. Once the children have reached this secure state they can then begin to learn higher-order movement and physical skills.

Children, however, cannot learn when they are not confident or if they are unhappy in their learning context. Those, for instance, who are not physically competent on entering pre-school will not choose to climb up a climbing frame if they are unsure of their own bodies or if physically competent children are already bustling about on it. Similarly, children who have not been afforded the pleasure of playing freely in the outdoors will not choose to be there, and conversely, those who have come from a street environment will not feel happy about being indoors (Tizard 1976). So if we believe that the learning process consists of the active engagement of the learner, it is important that educators are fully aware of each child's situation and that they become keen observers of children's movements. Meanwhile, children in their turn have to learn to adapt to their environment.

There can be little doubt that children are learning all the time, and that most of this learning in the early years is connected to movement of various types. Davies (1995: 1) has written that there is no divisibility between movement and human functioning, and that movement is such a fundamental part of human lives it is often unclassified in early learning situations. Edwards and Knight (1995: 25) have suggested that we know very little about the mechanisms and processes of children's learning and that we can only work with the 'best guesses' presented to us by research psychologists. Traditionally, a broad framework of how children learn has been based on Piagetian theory and many researchers have focused their attention on the stages through which children are thought to proceed in developing their understanding and their learning readiness (Piaget, Inhelder and Szeminska 1960, Anderson and Cuneo 1978). This type of research, however, is not always applied to education in the pre-school setting, particularly in relation to the physical education of children. I would agree with Edwards and Knight when they suggest that research psychologists such as Piaget, for instance, were concerned more with the nature of knowledge, and never asked educational questions. Clearly the essential questions which adults in pre-schools should ask themselves about children's movement and motor skill learning are 'What do I know about this learner?' 'What type of activity should I provide for this learner?' 'What do I want the child to learn from this activity?' and 'What can I do to assist this learning?' Teachers should also be aware of the previous experiences which each child brings to the learning situation and, as a result, structure both the environment and their teaching strategies so that each child acquires the physical competence to fulfil the task which the teachers wish the child to achieve. It is very important, then, that once children reach statutory school age, teachers should have a detailed report from the pre-school setting which the children have attended which gives information about the experiences which each child has had and their physical competencies. Unfortunately, it is not quite as simple for infant teachers to provide a selective programme for each child as it was in the pre-school setting and that is why the pre-school education of the physical child is so important. I would suggest that the pre-school years are the crucial time for children to become physically confident and competent in using their own bodies in order to be able to fulfil the demands placed on them in later life. Children who are normal should enter the pre-school setting with several basic biological movement competencies, and once they have become secure in the pre-school it should be possible for educators to check these movement competencies and set about providing each child with specific movement activities to enable them to reach a normative biological status. We can no longer leave this learning to the osmosis approach in which children select their own play and as a consequence their own learning activities. In their detailed observations of children in nursery schools, many researchers (Berry 1993, Cooper 1972, Hutt 1972, Wetton 1989, 1995) have shown how important the presence of the adult is in the children's choice of gross motor activities (and for some children, for all activities). It is clear from these observational studies that for many children interaction between children, activity and adult, is crucially important in motor skill learning. If this is the case, then it cannot be emphasised too strongly how important it is for educators to assess the children's status on entry to pre-school.

As was stated earlier, children are both bio-cultural and bio-social individuals. Often they can be prevented from accessing learning situations because they do not have either the essential social or cultural skills to accomplish this (Osborn, Butler and Morris 1984). Some children will have had experience of exuberant play in their toddler days at home. They will have had the opportunity to be involved in boisterous games with other children, to play in mud, to get wet running in and out of garden hoses, to run up and down hills, to shout, to giggle and to laugh. Others will have played in empty buildings, climbed on the wrecks of cars, jumped off walls and fences and learned to run fast. Some children, however, will have been restricted from taking part in these kinds of movement practice. They may not have siblings and neither may they have had an opportunity to play with other children either in the home or outside the home setting. Undoubtedly, some will have been encouraged to play quietly and offered a restrictive diet of fine motor play, whilst others will have led sedentary lives in front of the television. Research is already showing the impact on children of some of these different types of cultural nurturing. Children who receive day care outside the home, for instance, are more likely to be socially capable when playing with peers (Marino and Fiese 1993), but are likely to be more aggressive than those reared in the home (Schwarz *et al.* 1974). If teachers are to focus on the learners as they acquire and attempt to improve their motor skills, then it is important that they know what children should be able to achieve as biological 3-year-olds. They should also know which motor patterns develop between the ages of 3–4 years and 4–7 years.

Initially, then, on entry to pre-school at 3 years of age, the majority of children should be able to perform the following.

Gross motor and locomotor skills

- Walk forwards, backwards and sideways (general body management);
- walk on tip-toes (balance);
- show a basic running style (general body management)
- climb up steps or a ladder with one foot leading, maximum step depth 21cms (bodily co-ordination);
- climb down a ladder, one foot leading, with hand support (bodily co-ordination);
- pivot round and round on feet (balance and control of body);
- walk up and down mounds (bodily co-ordination);
- jump up and down on the spot on two feet (strength and bodily co-ordination);
- jump a distance of 36cms (leg strength);
- jump down from one foot to two feet from a height of 45cms(agility and confidence);
- balance walk along a plank at a height of 18cms from the ground (balance);
- balance on one (preferred) leg for 4 seconds (balance);
- crawl through a barrel or drain-pipe (agility);
- climb through the lowest rungs of a climbing frame (agility).

Children should also be able to perform the following fine motor skills, although it must be accepted that some children will not have had the opportunity to handle some of these objects because of their cultural nurturing.

Fine motor skills

- Place three blocks (2.5cms–5cms in size) on top of each other (eye–hand co-ordination, and spatial ability);
- make a straight road with ten building blocks, having been shown an exact replica (eye–hand co-ordination and spatial awareness);
- affix a piece of construction apparatus to a hole in another piece (two-handed co-ordination);

- assemble a six-piece jigsaw (eye–hand co-ordination and spatial ability);
- paint a person with a head and two other body parts identifiable (eye–hand co-ordination and internalisation of representation);
- grip and make marks on a paper with a thick soft pencil (fine motor control);
- copy a circle;
- hammer shapes into a pegboard (manipulative strength and eye–hand co-ordination accuracy);
- make a ball with clay or playdough (manipulative strength and one and two–handed co-ordination);
- pour water from a jug with a spout into a large container (fine motor control);
- thread large beads on to a lace (two-handed co-ordination).

They should also be capable of performing the following.

Eye–hand and eye–foot co-ordination skills

- Catch a large ball thrown by an adult between their extended arms (eye–hand co-ordination);
- catch a small ball thrown by an adult between extended arms (eye–hand co-ordination);
- kick a standing ball forcibly (eye–leg co-ordination);
- pedal a tricycle along a wide chalked or painted line (eye–leg and eye–hand co-ordination);
- push a ball away from self across the floor surface (eye–hand co-ordination);
- pull an empty truck around obstacles (strength, eye–hand co-ordination).

All normal children should be able to perform the above tasks when they enter pre-school and should be targeted for special attention if they cannot accomplish them. Unfortunately, my observations of children in pre-school settings have shown conclusively that some children are not targeted for special attention if they cannot perform these tasks and suffer accordingly. Bruner (1980: 59–61), reporting on the findings of the Oxford Preschool Research Group, was critical of this lack of targeting. He concluded from his observations that adults placed too much emphasis on such things as management activity when they might have been more profitably occupied in both stimulating and targeting children through focused play and structured activities. If focused play and structured activities are offered, then each child can be assessed and those found to be lacking in some or all the motor capabilities required can be given the necessary attention. In some cases, children may only lack motor capability as a result of their home nurturing and they may quickly become competent. For example, some children may find fine motor tasks difficult mainly because they have spent much of their early life playing outdoors. Their eye–hand co-ordination is likely to be proficient, but often it is the type of task required which may be unfamiliar to them. For instance, if the teacher had asked them to pile three builder's bricks on top of each other instead of three plastic cubes, there may be no problem! For other children, it may take longer for them to achieve the desired goals. The important point is, that since research shows us that pre-school educational experience has a greater influence on conceptual maturity and fine motor skills than on vocabulary (Osborn 1981), it is surely important for all children to gain access to practice and for this essential element in children's educational development not to be left to chance.

Whilst the acquisition of fine motor skills is an essential element in all children's educational progress, for some children it is the acquisition of gross motor and locomotor competencies which is most likely to be neglected in pre-school situations. Children's lack of gross motor and locomotor competence can limit their confidence and they could, if not targeted, start on a downward spiral which will eventually lead to social problems in primary school playgrounds. Some of these children will not have had any experience of playing with other children and will just simply not know what to do to to gain access to shared play. Others, having learned access strategies, will quickly become outcasts if they do not have any physical competencies to enable them to take part.

There are many problems for children nowadays which frequently prevent them from becoming fully integrated into group activities. Children coming from different cultures, for instance, often have a dual problem, one being a lack of understanding of Anglo-Saxon play practices whilst the other will almost certainly be lack of language. I have a young Jordanian friend who, in her first week at pre-school, learned her first two English words, 'don't' and 'please'. Not only does this tell us much about the children and staff in her pre-school, but it also seems to suggest that she may have difficulty in joining in activities.

Sometimes the problems can be physical. For example, many children might have dyspraxia, a medical term now given to a condition in children who were formerly classed as 'clumsy'. Children with this condition have a co-ordination disorder which is related to balance and movement. In 1989 Groves suggested that 5 per cent of all school children experience motor problems and that there would probably be at least one child in each class who would seem 'physically awkward', or, as she termed the condition, 'clumsy' (Groves 1989: 130). The medical research charity Action Research (Waan and Mon-Williams 1996) has suggested that if this condition is recognised then specialist treatment should be sought as early as possible. Incidentally, it is a fascinating observation, made after studying and analysing metres of videotape, that there are children who ostensibly are normal but who are either slightly 'clumsy' or socially inept and are not tolerated if they show any deviation from normal playing styles. Yet other children who have been statemented and have visible special needs are tolerated. It will be interesting to receive other people's observations of this phenomenon.

Children, then, present various characters and physiques when taking part in pre-school education and need to be stimulated to develop their personal, social, physical, emotional and intellectual growth at their own rate of learning. In order that each child can progress in this way, the philosophy in pre-school education has been to provide a structured play environment where each child can choose to play. Where pre-schools make good quality provision and have a strong educational commitment to pre-school education, the children will be provided with a rich environment where they can choose to play. Such an environment would be carefully structured both indoors and outdoors with varied forms of play activities, so providing the children with an opportunity to practise their emerging motor patterns at their own rate of learning when they are biologically capable of achieving them. Where such good quality provision exists, it is highly likely that teachers will have certain learning goals in mind and will observe their children as they play to assess when they are ready to progress to the next set of learning goals. In some pre-schools however, whilst the quality of provision might be good, the observation of the children is not always of a similar standard. In situations where this occurs, this practice of free choice of play works for some children but not for others.

Some of the finest examples of motor learning would seem to take place within the free choice of play framework. A typical example I have witnessed recently was of a 4-year-old who was able to use an activity provided by her teacher to set her own learning goals and thereby develop and advance her own learning. She was triggered into action by the colourful layout in the indoor environment of an Edra system. As she was socially and physically competent, she quickly gathered others around her. All the children walked on the raised curved and straight pathways which the teachers had erected. The 4-year-old walked forwards and backwards, turned and stepped past others. Her peers struggled to balance and some stepped off the apparatus at regular intervals. A child with special needs enjoyed being with the the other children, and was tolerated. The 4-year-old girl meanwhile, was becoming more and more proficient and started to rearrange the layout so that it was more challenging for her, e.g., she extracted pieces from the layout to make a stepping-stone pathway where it was necessary to step from one obstacle to another. She placed the obstacles about 22cms apart. Finally, she planned a balancing task which the teachers had presumably thought to be too difficult – and for all the other children it was. The above is an example of the information processing model of motor learning working effectively. In theoretical terms, the learner had received an environmental cue, perceived what was required to complete the task, had assembled all the motor abilities stored in her movement memory and using all this, had set out to complete the task, using her stored motor information. She had then decided that the task was either too simple, or more likely that she was no longer stimulated by the environmental cue, and so had decided to change it. She could be described in Fitts and Posner terms as having reached the autonomous stage in her movement learning (Stallings 1982: 67–93).

Another example of free choice of play leading to self-initiated movement learning developed through an observation of five children in a nursery school. The children, led by one 3-year-old girl, decided that they would dress up in ballet skirts or cloaks. The girl asked a teacher if she could use the tape-recorder, chose a tape, put on the music and all five children danced to the music. My own observations of 3 and 4-year-olds has normally shown me that when the children dance to 'the tune of the teacher', they do not always express themselves in an artistic manner and often use only their arms and legs to move in response to a request to move to the music. Consequently, there is very little movement in the hips or the spine. In this self-initiated group movement session, these children showed a fluency in their movements and demonstrated an ability to use their bodies in both a dynamic and rhythmic manner which was outstanding. They exhibited light gentle movements, sometimes slow and sustained, sometimes controlled and sometimes free. They used flexible movements as they swayed and pirouetted to the music and as they moved from one part of the space to another. They did not demonstrate any quick sudden movements, nor strong or firm movements, and were not seen to move in a straight or direct pathway, but perhaps this was a result of the choice of music rather than the inability of the children to show this aspect of the dynamism of movement possibilities.

If it is possible for children to reach the standards given in these illustrations you might wonder at this stage why there should be any criticism of the free choice of play method of learning physical skills. You might also wonder what is considered to be good quality provision. After much observation of children in pre-schools it would appear to me that a mixed method of providing learning opportunities should be established as a regime for teaching physical skills. Undoubtedly, for some children, the free choice of play approach can be classed as good quality provision but for the vast majority of children, this is not the case. For instance, at the same time that I observed the children described above – and in the same nurseries – I saw other examples of children not being able to choose to play, children who could not put on their own wellington boots and were therefore denied access to the garden to dig and to splash in puddles, children who were overweight and overdressed and had on unsuitable shoes who could not climb further than the first rung of the climbing frame. I also saw children wandering about without purpose. It would seem very important that teachers should plan to implement a number of different strategies if all the children are to access the physical play which they need in order to learn the essential motor skills in pre-school which will allow them to develop and progress, both educationally and socially.

To this end, then, teachers should create a good quality environment both indoors and outdoors and make the following provisions for:

- free play and directed play opportunities;
- interventionist physical activities for groups of children;
- situations where they play with the children;
- structured learning activities in gymnastic activities;
- structured learning activities in dance;
- structured learning activities in games activities.

Once such environmental possibilities have been established and appropriate opportunities set up for learning to take place, then teachers will be in an excellent position to observe the children carefully, assess their emerging capabilities and record those skills which the children can perform autonomously. Wherever possible, too, those children who are observed to be underachieving should be targeted for special attention.

PLANNING ENVIRONMENTS

It is unfortunate that in some pre-school settings the outdoor environment is structured to enhance gross motor and locomotor skills whilst the indoor environment is structured to enhance fine motor skills. This would appear to be a practice which should be reviewed, particularly in relation to the points made earlier about the different home cultures which children come from and also because of that great British enigma – the weather!

THE INDOOR ENVIRONMENT

In many pre-schools, the provision for physical play and movement learning for young children is often varied and not always provided with the children's home environment in mind. This is especially true with respect to the provision for 'learning to move' and 'learning through movement' throughout the different pre-school settings of nursery schools, playgroups and reception classes in infant schools, often with the latter having the least provision of all. This is unfortunate since many observational studies have highlighted the need for children to be free to climb, to run, to chase and to be involved generally in rough-and-tumble activity.

Pre-schools themselves were once places where children could practise all their emerging physical skills. Sadly, however, more and more pre-schools are structuring their indoor environments in the style of reception classes, thus limiting their children's gross motor and locomotor play opportunities. Consequently, children in pre-school environments these days are more likely to spend a large part of their time on pre-National Curriculum fine motor co-ordination activities so that the nearest children get to experiencing any gross motor practice is probably in the excellent life corners which are set up to stimulate imaginative and creative play, or when building with large building blocks. Almost by way of compensation, many children create their own gross motor and locomotor practice by pretending to be cats or dogs and crawling about on hands and knees in the life corner, or 'flying' around the available space as Superman! Unfortunately, however, if proper provision is not included in planning, the crucial motor practice which is a pre-requisite for later pencil, computer key, instrument and reading co-ordination can be lost. Obviously, if the outdoor environment is always accessible to children then their needs can be met, but if, on the other hand, the doors to the outside are closed and only accessible for limited periods in each session then it would seem that children are almost being denied their right to move. Activity is essential to young children, for when they are variously involved and engaged in activities which give them practice in controlling their bodies, and using their bodies in different ways, they learn new concepts and advance their physical and cognitive skills. It must always be remembered that, at this stage, children are still learning through their bodies and to demand that they be static for long periods of time can only result in retarding their growth. Research tells us that many of the concepts they learn at this point in their development are linked to movement. Take the example of children's painting. Athey (1990) and Buckham (1994) have analysed children's paintings and concluded that children make sense of their world by painting the 'actions' which occur in them. Aubrey (1994) has written about the importance of the physical environment, which allows children to begin to recognise and use the properties of shape, and recognise relationships between shapes as they develop their mathematical understanding. It also seems certain that children learn much about number and seriation when they are involved in action songs and rhymes and learn about important mathematical concepts such as 'under', 'behind', 'in front', and so on as they climb on climbing frames and listen to the language of operations. Harlen (1985), in particular, has been a great advocate in promoting the notion that children develop their ideas about the scientific world from their earliest years. As they push, pull and manoeuvre tricycles, they begin to understand the laws of forces and motion. As they play on the see-saw and try to balance the body weight of their play partner they learn much about balancing mass, and they also begin to work out problems such as why they stop when they come to the bottom of the slide, or why they go faster when they adopt certain body positions. I am reminded, too, of a young 4-year-old friend who, having reached the top of the slide said, 'I am taller than you!'

So, if the outdoor environment is not constantly available, then the minimum requirement for indoor gross motor and locomotor play is as follows:

- the provision of a multi-purpose climbing frame (with a slide, and a balance bar attachment);
- the provision of toys with wheels;
- the provision of large building blocks;
- the freedom to walk about the establishment without restriction;
- a space and a suitable surface for rough-and-tumble play;
- a space for teacher-directed activities.

Where space is really limited, particularly in nursery and reception classrooms attached to primary schools, then the children should have access to the school hall, a facility which ought to be available to the children at least once every day. In order to develop essential competencies, directed teaching can be a successful method of helping children who do not know how to access free play, or who would not normally choose to be involved in locomotor and gross motor play. Before beginning activities, the children should strip down to vests and pants as they do in infant school since this will allow those who have come to pre-school in unsuitable clothing and footwear to become less restricted and more mobile. Changing for activities, incidentally, also gives the children another opportunity to practise a very important life skill, i.e., learning to dress themselves. It also gives them valuable fine motor and eye–hand co-ordination practice as they unbutton clothes and untie laces and unfasten buckles.

Those pre-schools which are committed to providing a good quality physical environment can build on the provision of the six elements suggested above by providing some of the following additional equipment:

- a see-saw;
- Edra play equipment;
- balance planks;
- tricycles;
- a rocking horse or tot rocker;
- cardboard boxes (and other packaging material);
- wheelbarrows, carts, trucks;
- a barrel or tunnel;
- soft play shapes and a mat;
- audio tapes and a tape-recorder;
- toys which develop co-operation with another child.

All equipment used for Physical Education activities should always be selected with both educational and safety considerations in mind. Nowadays, almost all recognised educational suppliers are fully aware of these safety and educational considerations and have created catalogues with a plethora of suitable apparatus and equipment from which teachers can choose (see resources section). Criteria for the selection of equipment should be primarily that it is free from sharp corners and edges, and the correct weight and size for the children's age and competencies. There should also be due consideration given to the children's leg length, and there should be no moving parts which might trap little fingers. Manufacturers are aware that equipment should be adapatable and that it should be capable of being easily stored, so that apparatus can be changed and added to, to create new challenges. This is particularly important, since children have been shown to prefer apparatus which they can adapt for their own creative play and which they can be allowed to erect along with the teacher. All the apparatus on the educational commercial market is produced in strong colours to make it attractive and to help children with colour recognition. There is also a tendency to make it out of heavy-duty noiseless plastic, which is understandable because of considerations of durability, colour and cleaning. However, there are still some specialist Physical Education apparatus manufacturers in the marketplace who use wood and metal in the construction of their equipment and so a good recommendation would be a mix of all these materials, if only because children can then be exposed to different tactile experiences when handling the equipment provided for them.

As far as the positioning and layout of these pieces of equipment is concerned, there is an obvious need for careful planning. A prime consideration in planning should be that there is enough space around each piece of apparatus for children to pass by safely, particularly where rough-and-tumble is taking place. There should be open spaces for children to move at speed. It is not necessary to have all the apparatus out every day or even every week. Even 4-year-old children, working in what could be classed as the finest Physical Education environments, have become bored with the layout and the equipment being used, either because of familiarity after five or six terms of play or because they have become physically competent. In cases such as this clearly a new challenge is needed!

THE OUTDOOR ENVIRONMENT

OFSTED (1993) has been critical of the lack of outdoor play experiences for children in pre-school settings, particularly for 4-year-old children in reception classes. Since outdoor play has always been considered to be an important factor in the motor learning of children (McMillan 1919, Isaacs

1938, Waxman and Stunkard 1980, Moyles 1989, Klesges *et al.* 1990, Baranowski 1993), perhaps we should consider how children learn to move in the outdoors and how best to plan for it.

Many parents are no longer secure about letting their children play unsupervised outdoors in the home setting. Even though children are no less safe than they were twenty years ago (Home Office 1995), parents are nervous about allowing their children the freedom to gain the social skills, the movement skills and the independence which they themselves learned in the outdoors when they were pre-schoolers. As a result, many children spend considerable amounts of time indoors.

However, research shows us that as children move out of the toddler stage they cannot develop either their gross motor skills or their movement skills in the restricted environment of the home. This would be a serious situation for children if pre-school provision was not available to them, because if pre-school provision is well planned and delivered, then adequate physical and social compensation should be the result. Nevertheless, it is a matter of some concern that a new generation is being raised in a society where an active lifestyle is not possible outdoors close to home, a lifestyle essential to the health and well-being of these same children when they become adults.

Research from the *National Study of Health and Growth* into children of 5–11 (Department of Health and Social Security 1995b) offers more worrying information when it shows that children overall are becoming taller, heavier and fatter. Similarly, a report from the Chartered Society of Physiotherapists (1995) indicates that in a survey which they conducted one-third of the children were found to be less fit then they used to be ten years ago. Both these groups are concerned to ensure that children are educated from their earliest years about the importance of good quality exercise in the search for good health in their adult years. It is another concern that children should have a healthy and happy childhood. Unfortunately, some findings are beginning to show us that many obese and unfit children are more inclined to be bullied or/and ridiculed in childhood (Gray and Buttriss 1993).

It would appear, then, that the development of a healthy and active way of life is important for a number of reasons:

1 The prevention of overweight and obese bodies. The prevalence of overweight and obesity increases with age. Ten per cent of males and 13 per cent of females are considered to be overweight or obese by the age of 7 (Department of Health and Social Security 1995b: 1).
2 Strengthening bone. Exercise is more effective than calcium in increasing bone density (University Medical School, Rotterdam).
3 Preparation for puberty. If children are to have strong bones by puberty, bones need to be stressed to lay down calcium.

4   Prevention of disease in later life. Obesity in adults can increase the incidence of diabetes, mellitus, high blood pressure, strokes, coronary heart disease, arthritis, gall bladder disease, respiratory infections and so on.
5   Healthy growth and development.
6   Gross limb–eye co-ordination, and fine motor co-ordination.
7   Development of control and mobility.
8   Development of conceptualisation.
9   Strengthening muscles.
10 Increasing manual dexterity.
11 Social, emotional and moral development.
12 Enjoyment. If children enjoy the activity they are encouraged to take part and be active.
13 Development of concept of self. Enjoyment of active pursuits leads to the development of confidence and self-concept.

So teachers who understand the importance of physical activity in the development of children's movement learning and who believe that it is important to teach children as early as possible about the importance of an active lifestyle will plan the outdoor environment carefully. Ideally, the outdoor area should always be a continuation of the indoor environment, which means that the doors to the outside area should always be open. Children like to be outside and have been observed to choose to play outside rather than inside when free choice of play sessions are part of the curriculum. Undoubtedly, it is more natural to allow children free access to the outdoors rather than have a 'timetabled' half-hour playtime. Wherever possible, then, the outdoor environment should be as natural as possible. The following questions should form a framework when planning the provision of an outdoor environment.

• What do we know about the children?
• What are our learning goals?
• What is our role?
• How do we make the equipment and the environment safe for the children?
• Which types of equipment are most likely to stimulate most motor learning and encourage the development of emergent motor patterns?
• Which types of surface will produce the most learning and the most enjoyment?
• How can we make the environment stimulating and challenging?

What do we know about the children?

Every pre-school or nursery class will have children with different abilities and aptitudes within its midst, so it is not possible to be definitive about the 'make-up' of a particular class. Clearly, however, the differences which exist between the children can have a considerable effect on what can be offered, and so it is important to be able to recognise such differences and take them into account when planning programmes. Initial consideration should always be given to the age, ability and sex of the children in question and the learning goals which they will be expected to achieve, but special arrangements will also have to made for those children with disabilities and those coming from different cultures and for whom English is a second language. Disability, incidentally, often means children with particular motor learning problems and who require special planning, e.g., suitable equipment and staffing which could include in some situations the services of a paediatric physiotherapist.There may also be a case for providing particular help for those children who are physically gifted. At a practical level too, teachers might want to consider whether a policy of dividing the children into two age-group classes would give them – and the staff – better opportunities to make progress. There have been many examples of good practice emerging, for instance, where the older children attend in the mornings whilst the younger ones attend in the afternoon. As far as the presence of children from other cultures is concerned, they often bring their own styles of play into the pre-school and some preparatory planning may be needed to accommodate this. It is often a good idea to consult the social services or community leaders about special cultural needs and interests should this situation arise. Sometimes all that these children lack is to be 'keyed' into the language of operations used so frequently by nursery staff and often only need to be shown what to do by visual example through body language or initially with simple word accompaniment. Many children learn the English language in this manner and the value of the use of body and action cues should not be underestimated.

Finally, a word about boys in pre-school classes. Observational studies (Cooper 1972, Wetton 1980, Millar 1971) show clearly that boys have a need to be involved in what has been termed, 'rough-and-tumble play', which is a difficult activity to classify, hence the term used. Outdoors, for example, they might be seen to be rolling on grass, or wrestling with each other or simply falling down for fun! There is no recognisable pattern to this kind of physical activity but it often occurs after a spell of concentrated fine motor activity. Boys need this kind of play indoors if it is not available outdoors and it is as important to their development as playing in the 'life' corner seems to be for girls. Observation of children at play would also lead to the conclusion that boys prefer to be involved in gross motor and locomotor play outdoors whilst the majority of girls are more likely to prefer to be involved in creative play, imaginative play and fine motor co-ordination activities.

What are our learning goals?

All children of pre-school age need to be active for reasons listed earlier. The quality of their involvement will depend to a great degree on the involvement of their teacher and so play opportunities will need to be well planned. Eight learning goals for successful teaching outcomes are suggested below:

1   To develop an understanding of the importance of being active. Teachers should involve themselves in organising running, chasing, jumping and hopping activities with the children, resulting in displays of 'puffing and panting', so that they can talk to children as they move and begin to make them aware of the results of physical activity on the heart and lungs.
2   To develop the children's body awareness. Teachers should construct some body awareness activities such as stamping feet, wiggling fingers and thumbs, turning wrists, circling arms, taking long steps, walking on tip-toes and heels, stretching arms, legs and spines, bending knees, elbows and hips.
3   To ensure that the children develop their spatial awareness and their eye–hand and eye–leg co-ordination skills. Teachers should make provision for the children to pedal and manipulate tricycles, trucks and other wheeled toys and to practice manoeuvring the toys into and out of spaces and around objects.
4   To ensure that the children develop their bodily co-ordination. Teachers can play with groups of children as they practise jumping up and down on the spot or running to kick a standing ball, as they skip, and as they run and jump over objects. Teachers can observe children as they choose to climb up and down steps and climbing frames.
5   To develop the children's agility. Teachers can observe and assess the children's performance as they choose to play on stepping stones, to climb through climbing frames, to slide down slides, to crawl through pipes or barrels or tunnels. Teachers can play with children as they run around obstacles and as they run and collect objects which teachers have placed in a line on the ground.
6   To help the children develop their fine motor skills as they dig in the sand, carry objects from one place to another, throw balls, open and close doors, pour water from container to container, brush water on fences and walls, screw screws into wood, manipulate bats of various sizes and catch balls thrown by adults.
7   To encourage the children to be independent for example, self-selection of toys and play partners, problem-solving and negotiation.
8   To encourage co-operation. Teachers can provide large, wheeled toys which can only be manoeuvred by two people.

The teacher's role

The teacher's role is very important in helping children to achieve the learning goals listed above. As with other aspects of teaching young learners, teachers must become both expert observers and expert evaluators. Observation must be made of children in various situations, followed by an evaluation of the learning taking place at that particular time. The whole process should then set new goals in place for the children, the ultimate aim being the achievement of progression. Initial observations will also allow teachers, even at this early stage, to deduce that some children are more physically competent than others.

Through their observations, teachers will have seen many of their children playing in the outdoor environment either with, on or around various pieces of equipment. They will see that many children play alone, whilst some children spend time negotiating for a turn with a favourite piece of equipment, and once having got it will not part with it until similar negotiations have taken place or, more likely, an adult has intervened! Other children can be seen pedalling tricycles back and forth, learning to co-ordinate pedalling and steering, to negotiate obstacles and to reverse and turn. Others will be seen to run and jump suddenly or may be pushing and pulling a truck to steer it with their feet, repeating the same manoeuvres until they are proficient. All the time concentration will vary but, for the most part, most of the children will be able to work independently, with a definite goal in view from which they will not easily be distracted.

To help teachers with their work of assessing and evaluating, it would be worthwhile referring to the motor learning model of Fitts and Posner (1967) mentioned earlier in this chapter. This is a model which identifies the stages which children go through as they approach, in this case, the physical tasks before them. Like all researchers and observers of motor skill learning practices and models its fundamental message is that the single most important factor in motor learning is practice. For the children characterised above, for example, the constant repetition of the skill eventually enables them to perform their chosen skill effectively. At the outset, they have chosen an activity and are considered to be in what Fitts and Posner suggest is the 'cognitive phase', i.e., children who have focused on a particular action or skill with the intention of enjoying it and who will improve by practising it. Furthermore, their behaviour would suggest that they may have displayed higher cognitive processes and capabilities than their peers and for them, as can be observed, the pre-school environment is sustaining their learning needs. Such children as these will probably move confidently on to the next phase – 'associative' – as described by Fitts and Posner, where they can produce the learned skill consistently without seeming to think about it, until eventually, if we were to use the example of tricycle riding, they will be able to pedal the tricycle whilst seeking more challenging routes. The physical act of pedalling the tricycle will become autonomous because the skill is established in the child's motor memory.

However, it will be possible to observe other children who can be seen cruising about in the outdoors spending only short amounts of time sampling different activities. Children such as these do not seem to be able to move into the 'cognitive' phase mentioned above. Even if they can manage to negotiate a turn with a tricycle, they never seem to be in the position where 'practice makes perfect' simply because they do not concentrate on the skill-learning task for long enough! They do not seem to apply any cognition to the task in hand, neither do they seem to know what it is they want to learn. Children like this, who flit around from task to task, will need some adult input if they are to learn any effective motor skills. Teachers should ask themselves whether they need to give them some direction so that they know how to practise a task, or at least give them an objective which will motivate them, e.g., try to pedal round two objects placed 5 metres apart. Since Fitts and Posner argue that practice won't make perfect if the learner is not motivated to practise the task, teachers in this position should consider making some suggestions and setting some challenges. There are, of course, a minority of children who rarely settle at any activity at all and wander aimlessly about the outdoor environment on the periphery of all the activities and who, unless a keen-eyed observer notices them, can deploy the most advanced and intricate avoidance tactics imaginable. Perhaps they represent the greatest challenge of all!

All of the examples so far indicate that children choose to play and to develop their motor skills in different ways and that the environment which is structured for them offers an opportunity for them to develop at their own rate of learning. Or does it? Teachers should have no concerns about the children who are completely competent both socially and physically. They will always be able to negotiate their way into any situation and almost demand any toy they choose. Invariably they are completely independent in attending to their own needs and in choosing activities. They can even initiate play situations and involve others in them, often conversing with adults and communicating their needs and desires confidently and competently. They can use adults to their own advantage. On the other hand there are groups of children who may not succeed in the free choice of play environment. For these children the provision of a carefully structured and motivating environment has not had the desired educative effect and it is for these children that early years educators should have concerns. Frequently this is because such children have visible or non-visible needs which present themselves in various ways. Some children may be physically disabled, some may have learning difficulties, others may be socially inept or emotionally unstable. There are many variations of each of these four groups of conditions. The teacher and nursery assistants are central to the success, happiness and general well-being of all children but for children with special needs the attitude of professional staff and all assistants is crucial. Support is especially important if special needs children are to be accepted by other children in the class, as well as for the development of their own particular self-worth and self-esteem. In terms of identification, the most obvious mani-festations of special needs are those children who suffer from such conditions as cystic fibrosis, asthma, Down's Syndrome, epilepsy, limb disablement, diabetes, speech problems, mildly affected cerebral palsy, and the maladjusted. Those who are less likely to be identified are those who are slightly maladjusted, the mildly visually- and hearing-impaired children and most of all, those children who have been diagnosed as 'clumsy'. Children with English as a second language will need support too. There are also those children who are least likely to be identified as having special needs but who may need special attention if they are to achieve the eight learning goals suggested earlier. These children are often not identified because many of their presentable behaviours are not obvious, i.e., if a child falls down in the playground, it will be some time before the combined staff and helpers begin to chronicle the incidents and assemble a case study of frequent accidents. Similarly, children who often bump into large apparatus or who wobble off gymnastic benches are more likely to be assessed as having a behavioural problem than a motor deficiency problem. Then there are those children who adopt avoidance strategies to cover up their perceived problem. Examples of avoidance strategies would be when the children choose to stand as far away from the teacher as possible during class activities so that there is less chance of the teacher noticing them when the children are required to perform large and fine motor skills. Another example would be when the children arrange to miss their turn when working on large apparatus, so that their motor deficiency is not noticed. The children merge into the crowd and by being quiet and non-disruptive the busy teacher does not always notice that the children have identifiable motor or sight-related co-ordination problems. It will be especially important for nursery staff to identify such children and ensure that, as they move around the nursery, an assessment is made of their capabilities so that learning strategies can be structured to help their progress. Several researchers (Gordon and McKinley 1980, Brown 1987, Sugden and Keogh 1990) have suggested intervention strat-egies to assist such children which are fairly easy for staff to put into practice, since most of them propose that the child should decide with the teacher what he/she would like to accomplish. Both teacher and child then work together to try to achieve it. An example of such negotiation might be that the child would like to learn to ride a tricycle. First of all, the teacher would ensure that the child has access to a tricycle and would help him/her to understand the motor elements involved in the task. Next, the with the task each day until he/she had reached an autonomous state. Finally, the child would be encouraged to seek a new learning goal until the staff considered that at least he/she had gained some success in each of the learning goals 2, 3, 4 and 5 before working on 6, 1, 7 and 8 (see page 22). A variation of this strategy might be for some children to work together in groups – with professional staff supervision – on the same learning goal. In this way, the self-worth of all the children would be protected.

At the other end of the spectrum, there are some children who will be able to demonstrate higher-order cognitive skills in the outdoors in relation to the acquisition of motor skills and who will often display similar abilities indoors. Often there is a small percentage of children who are very capable of performing complex gross motor and locomotor skills which would not disgrace the gymnastic performance of a 10-year-old, nor the dance performance of an 8-year-old. However, it is worth remembering that very, very few pre-school children can demonstrate the eye–hand or eye–foot co-ordination skills which are the hallmark of a 6-year-old. Some motor patterns depend so obviously on biological development and the supportive teaching of an adult that pre-schoolers could not possibly learn them in a free choice play situation. It is for this reason that teachers should consider making a place for stuctured play and teacher-directed activities in their work with pre-schoolers. Suggestions on how to do this are given in the next chapter and teachers may find them useful in providing a foundation and a guide when planning both interventionist and progress-ive activities for their teaching. Nevertheless, the teacher's role does include an essential requirement, which is to assess the children's perform-ance and to check whether the learning goals have been achieved. The following list is offered as an assessment check-list for those who need a guide to know which gross motor and locomotor skills children should be able to achieve at the end of the pre-school phase of their education.

To assess balance

• Stand still with eyes closed for 10 seconds;
• stand on one leg for 10 seconds;
• walk forwards along a chalked line (3 metres long by 5 cms wide);
• walk backwards on the line for 2 metres;
• hop along the line for 3 metres, first on one leg and then on the other;
• walk on tip-toe along the line for 4 metres;
• walk along a balance bar (16cms high by 10cms wide).

To assess bodily co-ordination

• Jump in the air from two feet to land on two feet;
• run and kick a stationary ball;

- climb up steps or climbing frame with alternate feet leading;
- five or more continuous skipping steps;
- run and jump over five objects (15cms high by 45cms apart), alternate foot leading.

To assess agility

- Crawl through a tunnel, barrel or pipe headfirst all the way;
- climb on a climbing frame with confidence (up, along, through);
- run fast with fluid style around an object placed 5 metres away;
- run and pick up four bean bags placed at 2 metre intervals and place each one in turn into a basket at the starting point;
- run in and out of six objects placed in a straight line (50cms apart) on both the outward and return journey.

To assess eye–hand co-ordination

- Roll a ball to an adult kneeling 3 metres away;
- kick a ball from a standing position at a target;
- pedal a tricycle around three objects placed 2 metres apart;
- throw a bean bag towards a target placed 3 metres away;
- catch a ball thrown by an adult;
- bounce a ball six times in succession.

To assess strength

- Pull a truck in and out of two obstacles placed 3 metres apart;
- load a truck with several bricks until the child feels it is full and stable;
- pull the loaded truck around two obstacles placed 3 metres apart;
- push the loaded vehicle along the same route.

How do we make the equipment and the environment safe for the children?

Safety has become a very important facet in pre-school education and all teachers have a 'duty of care' to provide both safe equipment and a safe environment for children. The premises of those who provide pre-school provision outside local education departments are inspected on a regular basis by Local Authority Inspectors who work to nationally agreed criteria. It would seem appropriate then for pre-school establishments to be guided wherever possible by this team of helpful specialists, many of whom are former Physical Education specialists. For further help, nursery schools operating within the state education system would be well advised to refer to the BAALPE publication *Safe Practice in Schools Physical Education* (1995) which gives detailed information on the provision of safe equipment and safe environments for physical activities.

Which types of equipment are most likely to stimulate most motor learning and encourage the development of emergent motor patterns?

Earlier in this chapter some indication was given about ways to ensure that children's emergent motor patterns develop effectively, but no specific suggestions have yet been made about the type of equipment which is likely to stimulate motor learning. Many pieces of equipment have been used in pre-school settings over the years, to such an extent that they have developed into traditional favourites when it comes to stimulating movement practice and motor learning. The following list of equipment has been compiled from observing the use of pieces in various pre-school settings:

- climbing frame with the capacity to be used for climbing up, through and down, sliding down (feet or head leading);
- large blocks which can be manoeuvred by the children (to build with, to jump over, to pull, to jump from);
- trucks and other types of vehicles which can be steered, pedalled, pushed, pulled and loaded;
- vehicles and toys which encourage shared movements with another child;
- tunnels, barrels and pipes;
- balls and bats of various sizes and targets/receptacles to aim at and throw into;
- obstacles and mounds to steer vehicles around;
- bridges, walls, mounds, stepping stones and balance bars to balance on;
- sand to dig, pour, move, pile;
- water to paint with, to pour (to paddle in, to throw, to splash – in warm weather!);
- junk materials to encourage creative play;
- clothes to encourage vigorous imaginative play (running, jumping, hopping, swooping, skipping, chasing, galloping);
- boat, caravan, playhouse, garden shed (all with relevant furniture and tools) and opportunities to play inside and outside.

Which types of surface will produce the most learning and the most enjoyment?

It is important for teachers to consider which types of surfaces are safe and will provide most enjoyment for children's play. There are many possibilities and variations. Typically state school pre-schools have had access to a hard surface and grassed surface but there are many ways that even the most basic provision can be made more exciting and challenging. Some schools have been able to do this, for example, by adding mounds to run up, down and around, or by having set groups of bushes in soil and covered them with bark chippings so that children can crawl under them. Other schools have provided gentle hard-surfaced slopes over which tricycles can be pedalled. An attractive variation is where hard surfaces are given road markings so that children can practise walking across zebra crossings, wait in their cars for the 'lollipop person' to allow them to proceed or drive their tricycles along marked roads. Any 'created' area with a mixture of differing tactile surfaces such as grass, sand, bark chippings, paving stones, stepping stones, energy-absorbent rubber or surfaces which are raised to produce slopes, platforms and mounds provides exciting possibilities for children's play and learning.

How can we make the environment stimulating and challenging?

In planning the outdoor environment, the last task for teachers is to make it both stimulating and challenging.

Ideally, to start with, it should have many of the surfaces suggested earlier and so, in the planning stage, it would be important to consider making provision for stretches of ground space where the children can run freely or where adults can become involved in directing the children's learning. There is no doubt that surfaces which are varied add challenge and stimulation to children, so that steps leading to raised grassed areas, winding pathways which children can walk and skip along and mounds and trees to run around and hide behind are ideal for youngsters' development. The same is true where hard surfaces are marked out as roads with curved pathways or roundabouts. Sometimes it may even be possible to build bridges to challenge children even further! Equipment is often useful in helping to create exciting layouts, e.g., tyres, while the odd disused boat would be a real challenge to young children if they have to work out how to climb out of it! Blocks, ropes, ladders, etc. have all been shown to stimulate children's thinking and to challenge the development of their spatial and bodily skills. An ideal environment should also contain fixed equipment and many teachers already ensure that fixed equipment is constantly available in areas which they have created for children's physical activity. The most common provision nowadays is of slides, climbing frames and sand-pits, but many children do have access to houses or boats, caravans or forts, and fences to paint with water. 'Non-fixed' equipment which teachers might consider using from time to time would be that which might be relatively new to children, for example, a tent, a paddling pool, a bouncy castle, a large squashy mat, or tunnels, barrels and pipes. The key to the successful use of the 'hardware', however, must always lie with the teacher.

Those teachers who know both how to maintain the children's interest and how to motivate and stimulate them into reaching the learning goals expected of them are, in most cases, doing this by demonstrating two 'models' of organisation, both of which rely on teachers being able to create both a supportive environment for the children and knowing when to deploy new equipment in the environment. The first 'model' is characterised by the provision of 'new' pieces of equipment at strategic times during the year, when teachers judge that the children are ready to develop higher-order skills. It is also built on the belief that familiarity is vital if children are going to follow through any schemas which they are in the process of developing. Teachers who use this model as a method of proceeding believe that the whole environment within the nursery should remain constant for periods of time. The research which has led to this thinking has been developed by Athey (1990: 51) who has shown that children can be observed to be apparently obsessive in playing using one action which embraces bodily, dynamic and spatial schemas, e.g., children who regularly ride a tricycle around a roundabout time after time after time, or who climb up and down a climbing frame endlessly without seeming to tire of the action. Such children, it is argued, could be in the process of developing a schema, and if the tricycle or the climbing frame was not available in the same place in which it was the day before, they could become confused and developmental patterns could be interrupted.

The second 'model' is characterised by teachers providing different pieces of equipment each day so that the focus for both teacher and child can be either one particular piece of equipment or one type of activity. Here, the intended outcome is for the teacher to devise a variety and range of learning tasks and goals for children and to monitor their individual progress. Challenge and stimulation are thus created by a daily change in the use of the equipment within the environment as each day the children are offered different tasks and learning opportunities. An example of how this might work is given below.

Day One

On the first day, no equipment would be put out at all and all the activities would be adult-directed. Groups of children would be offered dance, action songs and rhymes, gymnastic activities and circle games. Those children with special needs, including those 'gifted' children within the group, would be gathered into small groups for special attention.

Day Two

On the second day, the adults would put out large balls and bean bags for the children to play with alone, in twos or threes, or with the adults.

Day Three

On this day, the children could choose to play on the fixed equipment or to run, jump and chase anywhere in the area.

Day Four

On the fourth day, the traffic layout could be erected. Cars and tricycles, trucks, trolleys and other vehicles would then be offered for the children to use. The adults could involve the children in role-play activities connected with traffic situations.

Day Five

On the final day, spades, paintbrushes, rakes, buckets, hammers, saws, screwdrivers, wood and workbenches together with fantasy play could be provided. Also, the focus on this day could be on small animals, plants, flowers and tree care.

In this type of organisation, children do not become overfamiliar with their surroundings or the equipment, nor with the people who are working with in the organisational set-up. There is also a new challenge every day. For teachers, it is a valuable way of exploring varying forms of curriculum organisation and teaching techniques.

Both of the teaching 'models' discussed have been shown to be effective when working with children in the early years of their education. They do, however, rely on teachers being knowledgeable about how children acquire physical and associated skills, as well as having an ability to observe, assess and evaluate children's perfomances. Where teachers have this knowledge and ability then the pre-school environment created will indeed be both challenging and stimulating.

Chapter 3

Nursery class activities for the primary school hall

Generally speaking, nursery school staff value the importance of those aspects of learning concerned with the physical development of their children. Where good quality of provision exists for this physical development one would expect to find them not only providing a rich programme of fine motor skill activities, but also ensuring that the children have a balanced programme of gross motor and locomotor activities as well. Such gross motor and locomotor activities are concerned with developing the children's physical control, co-ordination, mobility, awareness of space and others and, above all, increasing their motor confidence. Some staff also contribute to the children's developing creativity when they provide opportunities, for example, for dance. All of them, however, provide continuity in the normal processes of each child's developing physical self, and allow them to reach the new moving milestones as each normal stage is reached.

In some nurseries there is both a suitably large space and appropriate apparatus, in the indoor and the outdoor environment, for children to play with a purpose. Often, in the early months in nursery, play with a purpose can be achieved with minimal intervention from adults. Most children will have played and learned in this way at home, and will feel secure if allowed to build on similar experiences. However, those young children who have not had an opportunity to play freely with other children will begin to learn about sharing and taking turns as they play and will continue to add to their learning about the motor capabilities of their own bodies. All children can use this medium for developing both motor and social skills.

Unfortunately, however, many 4-year-old children are educated in classrooms attached to primary schools where indoor space is limited. These children will have to rely on a different planning approach in order to gain the motor experiences outlined above. Often schools in such situations plan teacher-directed Physical Education lessons in the primary school hall and head teachers who value the importance of the physical area of learning will include the 4-year-olds in the planning of the hall timetable. Other head teachers may allow nursery staff to teach in the hall when the primary school children are enjoying their morning playtime. All children who have little access to free choice of physical play in their nursery class should be able to use the hall each day so that they can be offered a regular and balanced programme of gross motor and locomotor activities.

Data from the National Study of Health and Growth in children aged 5–11 shows that children are overall becoming taller, heavier and fatter than were children of former generations (Wiseman 1995). Similar results can be found in the National Diet and Nutrition Survey of children in the age group 1.5 to 4.5 years of age (Gregory *et al.* 1995). Such developmental trends as these cannot just be ignored. It must be a matter of some concern that the number of children who are fatter than those in former generations is on the increase, particularly if the situation could be alleviated by reverting to a nursery programme which gives children a chance to be involved in vigorous physical activity at school. Equally as worrying is the growth in the number of children who are termed 'clumsy' (see page 67).

It is impossible to overestimate the importance which satisfactory motor development and motor skill acquisition has upon a child's ability to learn. Nor should such development be left to chance or to the choice of the children themselves. If children had better muscle control and better muscle tone it is certain that they would be able to function more effectively and have fewer motor control problems when expected to sit down and involve themselves in such fine motor tasks as writing and keyboard manipulation. All the research of developmental psychologists points to the fact that gross motor development precedes fine motor development and that awareness of the trunk and large parts of the body and their movement control precedes both awareness and control of the small parts of the body and fine motor control. It must be realised, too, that muscle tone is achieved by regular and constant movement repetitions of the muscles and that bone density is maintained by putting stress on the bones during movement. This being the case, it is of crucial importance that teachers consider it when creating a balanced Physical Education programme which will give all children the chance to develop both the motor capacities and activity habits which will undoubtedly form the foundation for a healthy life.What follows are some suggestions about how such a balanced programme should be constructed and how it might be implemented.

Two recently published documents are especially useful as starting points for the creation of such a programme. Both the Nursery Education Scheme *The Next Steps* (Department for Education and Employment 1996) and the School Curriculum and Assessment Authority (SCAA) document *Nursery Education: Desirable Outcomes for Children's Learning on Entering*

Compulsory Education, are seen by the Secretary of State for Education and Employment, Gillian Shephard, as 'critical to ensuring that nursery education is of good quality and provides a sound preparation for the National Curriculum' (Ofe 1996: 1). The SCAA document is particularly helpful and sets out six areas of learning for consideration, one of which is 'physical development'. Nursery teachers could do far worse than plan their curriculum content around the learning outcomes outlined in this document. The area of learning referred to as 'physical development' is described thus:

> These outcomes focus on children's developing physical control, mobility, awareness of space and manipulative skills in outdoor and indoor environments. They include establishing positive attitudes towards a healthy and active way of life. Children move confidently and imaginatively with increasing control and co-operation and an awareness of space and others. They use a range of small and large equipment and balancing and climbing apparatus, with increasing skill. They handle appropriate tools, objects, construction and malleable materials safely and with increasing control.
>
> (SCAA 1996: 4)

Another area of learning described as 'creative movement' is described in the documentation, and since this area includes a reference to dance, it would seem appropriate to consider it alongside 'physical development' in constructing a progressive programme for the National Curriculum. The SCAA document also states that children's progress will be at different rates and that individual achievement will vary. At the same time, however, it maintains that all children should be able to follow a curriculum which enables them to make maximum progress towards the stated learning outcomes. In order to achieve this, it would seem important both to recognise and take the advice given to us by those specialists who work regularly with children, which is that motor development and skill learning comes with regular and consistent practice, and that significant progress can be made if children are given a short daily period of activity rather than a longer period once or twice each week.

Children who only have access to the school hall for their physical activities should be offered a programme based on the three areas of study in the National Curriculum, i.e., games, dance and gymnastics, but before discussing the curriculum content for each of these three activity areas in detail there are some important educational considerations to examine. Dowling (1995), for example, reminds us of the importance of the child's introduction and earliest experiences in school and how powerfully these influence the child's attitudes to learning and subsequent achievements. Trained nursery staff, then, need to be well aware of the need to make sensitive and careful plans to ensure that children have a successful and supportive start. Thus teachers should consider talking to parents before the children start school and emphasising the central importance of physical activity. Parents can be shown the hall, the equipment and some photographs of children in action, and can be given a brief synopsis of the curriculum.The children themselves should also have the opportunity to make preliminary visits to the hall before starting to be active there. Most importantly, teachers should not be expected to cope with a nursery class alone, and an assistant should be available for all the activities as they develop.

Children come to nursery with a good knowledge of their bodies. In fact it is often the one thing which they know most about. They have been learning about their own movement milestones through a process of sensory motor practice where physical play has been mostly self-chosen and self-directed, so they come to school confident that they can do something in the physical area of learning. It is therefore important that curriculum planning starts from the moving milestones which they have already achieved and builds on this foundation. This may mean that in the initial stages the three areas of activity mentioned above should be merged so that the children can become familiar with their new situation.

When planning teacher-directed activities in the hall it is important for all staff who will be assisting and supporting the activities to be aware of any policies which the nursery has constructed in relation to philosophy, methods, content, the needs of children with special educational needs (including the gifted) and safety. Teaching auxiliaries, students, visiting pupils and parents should be included in this group.The general principles outlined below could form a useful checklist.

1 Check the school PE policy and/or guidelines.
2 Safety:
   (i)   check that the hall is free from hazards, for example, protruding shelves, pianos, music stands;
   (ii) check that everyone has removed all bits and pieces which might prove dangerous to others such as jewellery, including your own (a brooch or ring could scratch a child);
   (iii) check the children's clothing and footwear to ensure that clothes have no 'floating pieces' which may become a hazard and that where children are not working in bare feet, they have footwear with non-slip and flexible soles.
3 Focus on each child's abilities.
4 Encourage independence by making the children responsible for their own actions.
5 Be aware of specific problems which could occur. Some activities may be inappropriate for some children, for example, an epileptic child climbing too high on apparatus or an obese child becoming overtired.

6 Consider using a variety of approaches so that the children are fully aware of the skill which is being practised. Sometimes a demonstration by a child or the teacher can be effective whilst at other times a careful oral explanation with descriptive body language will have the desired effect.

7 Set suitable open-ended tasks so that each child can practice the skill at his/her own rate of learning.

8 Observe and analyse the process of the children's learning as they practise the required skills so that suggestions for adjustments can be made for a successful outcome.

9 Use language to assist learning. Adults can use language in a variety of ways, for example, to check understanding, to reinforce learning, to advance learning and to build self-esteem. Questions can be asked such as 'Which hand are you going to use? Have you chosen the left one?' or 'I like the way you did that, have you tried doing that sideways?' or 'You're doing your jump really well! May I ask you to show it to the other children?' and 'You worked very hard, didn't you? You've made your heart beat faster!'

10 Make sure that all language used, and all instructions, are clear, so that the children understand the purpose of the task and comprehend the adult's language.

11 The focus in all lessons should be on activity and action, but in the initial stages of a new programme of physical activity be aware of each child's energy expenditure, particularly if they have special needs. Sometimes children are so excited and enjoy themselves so much that a heart condition or an asthmatic condition are momentarily forgotten.

12 Make sure that all helpers are aware of the aims and objectives of the lesson.

I suggested earlier that children using the school hall for activities should be encouraged to strip down to vest and pants, as they will be expected to do in primary school, but unlike primary school children they can be allowed more time to practise this important life skill of undressing and dressing before and after Physical Education lessons. Adults can use this time very profitably to talk to the children as they undo buttons and untie bows and laces. Mathematical understanding can be developed as shoes are matched into pairs, whilst the foundation for numeracy can be reinforced as buttons are counted. Colours of garments can be discussed. Clothes can be folded and set in neat piles. New language can be developed as the names of garments are identified. The whole process can be a time when adults share interactive communication with children. The children will also have an opportunity to exercise their fingers and to develop fine and gross motor skills by being involved in this process. They can also be given enough time to practise these skills so that they become competent, which will add to their self-esteem and their sense of achievement, thus generating a positive feeling about their emerging manipulative skills and encouraging independence both at school and at home.

Once children are in the hall, my advice would be to proceed gently and slowly at first. The children will have new language to learn. They will probably not be conversant with the names of equipment, for instance, and words such as mat, bench and climbing frame might be new terms or might have different connotations in the new setting. Additionally, they will probably not be aware of the language of actions in which they will be expected to become involved – verbal directions such as 'make a circle', 'stretch up tall', 'face me' or 'find a space' will seem foreign to these new learners. Some children will almost certainly be unsure of some of the names of parts of their own bodies, such as 'hip', 'back', 'shoulder' and 'heel'. Many will be unused to responding to operational language related to body parts, for example, 'kneel up' or 'kneel down', 'lie on your back ', 'lie on your front', 'put your arms at the sides of your body' and so on.

Once the teacher feels that the children are at ease both with their environment and the language in use there, the first set of movement activity sessions should form an introductory programme and should be structured around the movement milestones acquired before school entry. Familiar action songs, action rhymes and ring games can be used at this point because all have the essential elements to involve children in locomotor movements concerned with walking, skipping and running, together with gross movements of the body concerned with many movements of different parts of the body.

There are numerous collections of such activities from which to choose, frequently available in books (Harrison 1992, Max de Boo 1992, Matterson 1969) whilst the Early Learning Centre shops also have a good selection of audio tapes of songs and music which teachers can use to support their activities. If children use known content, even in an unfamiliar environment, but with a well-known teacher, they will often develop more confidence in the initial stages of learning the new language generated in Physical Education sessions. An example of some of the titles which I have found useful are: 'Heads and shoulders, knees and toes', 'Incy wincy spider climbs up the water spout', 'Peter taps with one hammer', 'Ring o'ring o'roses', 'Here we go round the mulberry bush', or 'Follow my leader', where teachers can invent their own actions:

Everybody do this, do this
Everybody do this, just like me!
[The teacher does an action such as clapping hands or stamping feet.]
Everybody clap hands, clap hands, clap hands,
Everybody clap hands, just like me!

Action songs and rhymes and circle games, such as the ones suggested, which allow all children to move for most of the time, will undoubtedly fulfil many of the physical learning principles outlined earlier. At the same time, children will also be provided with opportunities to recognise the names of body parts and the language of both actions and operations, through being involved with their peers in a comfortable and non-threatening medium.

A final word at this point about organisation. The children will develop their understanding quicker if the staff use similar strategies in each lesson, e.g., the method for assembling should always be the same in the initial stages so that the children are not disorientated. One method is to start every session by forming a circle. I know that this in itself is not an easy manoeuvre to achieve! Some teachers have used the strategy of lining the children up with the teacher leading the line and a helper bringing up the rear. By doing it this way the teacher can encourage the children to follow the person in front of them. Another suggestion would be to get the children to hold hands in order to gain confidence for the first ring game and then drop hands and stand alone in the circle for activities which follow. Once the children seem able to complete an assembly in this way they can then start to be weaned on to other methods of 'control', e.g., one method might be to suggest that the children find 'a magic spot', first to sit on, then to stand on.

Incidentally, activities such as 'Simon says' or 'One finger, one thumb, keep moving', are useful for practising movement actions whilst standing on a magic spot! Another useful action rhyme is:

I am as small as a mouse (curl up small);
I am as thin as a pin (stand with arms at the sides of the body);
I am as wide as a gate (stand with legs and arms wide apart);
I am as tall as a house (stretch both arms high).

Once the children have become accustomed to the larger space, and some of the conventions of using it, and have grasped the fundamental knowledge of the language of operations, the merged pattern of activities can be judged to be over and both teachers and children can be expected to move on to specific activities in relation to games, dance and gymnastics.

GAMES ACTIVITIES

It is often difficult at this stage for 4-year-olds to move into games activities concerned with small apparatus skills, since they will not be developmentally ready to acquire them, nor will they be versed in using space for themselves or with others. Games activities should therefore consist of class games which the teacher controls and which the teacher and the class play together, e.g., 'What time is it Mr Wolf?' or 'Grandmother's footsteps', both of which can be played successfully with 4-year-olds. Games such as these lead on progressively from action songs. They also focus on fun rather than on competition and allow the children to receive the essential health element of vigorous activity without threatening their self-esteem by being declared winners or losers. Initially, then, the games element of the curriculum should be concerned with activities which are not competitive and which do not need any equipment, so that the children can have plenty of practice in running, stopping and starting, and changing direction with others in the general space available. Working in this way they will also be achieving one of the SCAA's 'desired learning outcomes', that of developing their awareness of space.

Children should also have many opportunities to begin to understand the special language of games. They should become familiar with directional language such as 'up', 'down', 'backwards,' 'forwards', 'right', 'left', 'sideways' and 'through', and positional language such as 'inside', 'outside', 'behind', 'in front', 'over', 'line', 'team', 'by a partner', 'circle', 'stand at the side of' and so on. They will also learn the nomenclature of gross motor actions and of the quality of those actions when they are asked to 'run quickly' or 'bounce softly'. At the same time, as new and challenging language concepts are being assimilated, children will also be absorbing some of the aspects of the learning outcomes which will be expected to be generated in the mathematics area of learning, particularly mathematical language and the practical use of number and number operations. Furthermore, games activities also provide teachers with innumerable opportunities for developing each child's social and personal development. Positive social behaviour can be actively encouraged by giving children the opportunity to help and support others, to praise effort and improvement as games are attempted and the children play together.

In the early stages, then, the aim of all games lessons should be to develop the children's locomotor skills, to help them to understand the terminology of games in a non-threatening medium and to provide enjoyable physical activities which will encourage children to form good attitudes to activity which will lay the foundations for healthy and social lifestyle patterns. What follows are some suggestions of how games lessons with 4-year-olds might be arranged.

All lessons should start with a warm-up consisting of fun activities such as 'Jack Frost', an activity in which the teacher asks the children to run, or walk or skip, but when he/she says 'Jack Frost!' the children have to stand still. This can be followed by a game concerned with moving all the body 'parts', e.g., 'If you're happy and you know it' or 'Simon says'. The skill input in these early lessons should focus on helping those children who have difficulty in performing the basic locomotor skills of running, skipping, walking and stopping with control. Each lesson can then be concluded with a class game which the teacher can control. In the early stages, lessons such as these can continue in this way for a number of weeks, until the teacher feels that the children are ready to begin to learn to play with games equipment and learn some of the basic skills associated with using it, together with games skill learning. The decision to move on to use equipment should be based on the teacher's observations of the progress the children are making in coming to terms with the work they are doing.

In introducing the children to equipment and in order to prevent superficial learning, it is advisable to introduce equipment one piece at a time. The humble bean bag is an excellent piece of apparatus with which to start! It is easy to grasp, is malleable when carried or placed on the body, it does not roll away when it is dropped and it is unlikely to cause damage to furniture and windows. As before, lessons should begin with a warm-up without apparatus. At this stage such warm-up activities can be based on simple games like 'Jack Frost' or the 'Bean game'. Those who have not played the 'Bean game' before will find it both simple and entertaining. The format consists of the teacher giving the children the name of a bean and the children completing an action associated with it, e.g., 'Jumping bean!' – everyone jumps up and down on the spot, or ' Runner bean!' – everyone runs around the space or 'Baked bean!' – everyone lies on the floor on their backs with their arms spread wide. When all the children are 'huffing and puffing' the teacher can then move on to the skill learning part of the lesson.

Games skills themselves are usually classified into three types, all of which involve the children in processing information:

1 *Closed skills*. Skills which are performed in a predictable, pre-planned environment, for example, throwing a ball into a basket.
2 *Open skills*. Skills which are acquired whilst the body or the target is moving in an unpredictable manner, for example, being in possession of a ball whilst running and throwing it to another moving person.
3 *Serial skills*: Skills which are between closed and open skills, for example, dribbling a ball with the feet or a stick through a space between two obstacles.

Initially the normal 4-year-old will only be capable, developmentally, of acquiring skills in the closed skill family.

During the early stages of the promotion of games skill learning, teachers have an important role to play, especially in knowing what the normal 4-year-old is capable of doing. It is obvious that should teachers not be aware of the 4-year-old child's capability, they could be asked to perform a task totally beyond them which could lead to unecessary failure. For example, a 4-year-old is not capable of catching a ball which another child has thrown, for a variety of reasons. First of all, the thrower will not yet have acquired the skill of throwing straight, so the receiver would have to use advanced visual perception to locate the ball in flight. Second, the receiver would have to assess the speed of the ball and its possible flight path, while, finally, the receiver would have to estimate not only where to move but how fast to move to a location where the ball could be caught. Altogether an extremely complex set of physical decisions for the average 4-year-old to make!

Initially, then, teachers should concentrate on teaching the following achievable skills in the order suggested:

1 carrying objects in the hands whilst (i) walking (ii) running;
2 carrying objects in the hands whilst walking and running around hoops and cones;
3 carrying objects on different body parts;
4 running and stopping with control on command;
5 running and jumping.

This should include the following 'sending' skills:

6 rolling a ball;
7 throwing a bean bag along the ground, then in the air upwards, then across a space;
8 kicking a ball;
9 throwing a ball, underarm, along the ground, then in the air, then across the space.

Since some of these skills will not involve the children in vigorous activity, teachers should consider alternating a footwork activity (3 or 4) with a manipulative activity (6, 7 and 9). They may also consider that some school halls are unsuitable for some of these activities, but if foam balls, or the new super-safe balls which manufacturers of sports equipment have created are used, there should be no damage to windows or pianos (see resources section). It is quite possible that there may be some children in the class who will have been involved in games skill learning whilst they were in their first year in nursery. In cases where this occurs, these children may be able to progress their skill learning to a higher level than that suggested in this progressive structure. Wherever possible, they should move on to the work which is suggested in Chapter 5 for Key Stage 1.

After a sustained introductory programme where the children have acquired finesse in the movement milestones contained in playing games using locomotor activities, it can be assumed that they are ready to learn new skills. Again, using the bean bag is an ideal way of starting these new skill activities. The children can be introduced to the bean bag through a series of guided activities selected by the teacher so that they understand the properties of this 'apparatus'. For instance, they should be told to hold the piece of apparatus first in one hand and then the other, and then be allowed to walk and then run whilst holding it. Bean bags can be used in a variety of ways to give the children confidence. They can be dropped on the floor and picked up, they can be carried on different parts of the children's bodies, they can be propelled across the ground with an underarm throw and be given by hand to another person. Activities such as these will help the children to establish some of the essential elements of acquiring the foundations of games skill learning.

A class game is a useful way of consolidating work with bean bags. A game such as 'Keep the basket full' not only enhances all the individual skill work which is developing, but is also great fun and good for confidence. Here's how it works. The teacher puts all the bean bags in a basket and stands near it. The game starts with the teacher throwing the bean bags to different places in the room; the children are told to retrieve them. The aim of the game is that if the teacher is to win the basket must be completely empty, and if the children are to win it must be kept full. This game can be played at the end of any series of lessons which are concerned with bean bags. The second lesson using the bean bag could be a repeat of the first one. The third lesson might then focus on the skills associated with running in space to collect and return bean bags. Again, this could be followed by the 'Keep the basket full' game. A possible variation to 'Keep the basket full' might be to ask the children to start from a magic spot, which can be imaginary or real (sequencing spots or mini space stations), and take four steps before placing their bean bag on the floor and returning to their spot. The teacher can then ask them to run and pick the bean bag up. Since manufacturers make bean bags in the four primary colours, teachers can put a basket in each of the four corners of the room and then ask the children to run and put their bean bag in the basket which corresponds to the colour of their own bean bag or ask all the children to choose a basket to put their bean bag in and so on.

Four-year-olds can also have fun if they are introduced to relays at this stage in their learning. A simple relay might develop as follows. Organise the children into teams of four who line up alongside each other. One child from each team is asked to run to the front of the team and to put their own bean bag in a basket, and then to run to stand at the back of their own team. Each child has a turn. A variation might be that the next set of teams take turns to retrieve a bean bag from the basket. There are many permutations to this simple formula. Admittedly, relay racing does not give each child maximum physical activity, but it does give all the children an opportunity to take turns, to be patient and to develop a sense of 'team'. It also, of course, generates much additional incidental activity when they jump up and down on the spot whilst waiting for their turn. Children also have an opportunity to develop their mathematical understanding and numeracy cognition, to say nothing of their developing social skills involving turn-taking and resolving such questions as who pushed in where!

DANCE ACTIVITIES

Dance activities give all children (including the disabled) an opportunity to work at their own level, and can be developed from the general introductory programme after a few weeks. Throughout the introductory programme, children will have become familiar with action songs and rhymes, so teachers can continue to use these for the warm-up at the beginning of each lesson. The rhythms associated with these rhymes can not only be explored in conjunction with dance but also with other appropriate areas of learning, e.g., music or language development. Similarly, the dance medium sometimes crosses into the area of drama, and wherever and whenever such 'cross-overs' occur, it would seem sensible to follow the mood of the moment and develop them. Where teachers adopt such strategies then a balanced creative programme of a cross-curricular nature should be the result. Undoubtedly, dance lessons can be a useful medium in helping the children to reinforce and extend the learning being established in the other areas of the curriculum. Nevertheless, the specific dance elements which contribute to the physical and creative development of the children must not be neglected. The aim in dance lessons, therefore, must be to offer children an activity in which to develop:

- control, co-ordination, balance and poise;
- the ability to listen and to respond in movement to various stimuli (voice, percussion and music);
- the ability to understand how to use their bodies to express moods and feelings.

The question then arises as to how best to teach dance.

Often, dance programmes for nursery school children are associated with a general theme which is being explored in the classroom. If teachers believe in the schema theories associated with the work of Athey (1990), where children eventually begin to make links in their learning and create schemas, then using a thematic approach to dance would seem to be a very reasonable way of teaching. It would also seem likely, as Athey suggests, that the early years curriculum would be more effective if it was planned on the children's interests rather than teachers arbitrarily choosing topics in advance. Since pre-school children are usually concerned with daily events and identifiable concrete experiences which interest them, and since their thinking and talking is almost always connected to the present moment, it is important that teachers choose themes which are associated with the children's concrete knowledge. Indeed, Donaldson (1978) argues that if learning is not embedded in concrete or familiar situations then children will almost certainly fail in their learning. Initially, then, themes such as: 'My body', 'Animals', 'People who help us' and 'Toys', could be the focus of learning, followed by themes concerned with 'Weather' and 'Transport'. As progress is made, 4-year-old children eventually become able to think and talk about past and future events in their own lives, and certainly begin to think about situations and problems which are not part of their own lives, a process which does develop during pre-school years. As and when this process occurs, i.e., when they begin to think about the past, they will begin to understand topics connected with, for example, 'Families', and with other habitats such as 'The Jungle', where they can locate animals which they have only seen in a zoo, in a book or in a film.

As far as the planning of individual dance lessons is concerned, it is important for teachers to provide a learning environment where all types of learners can be accommodated. Undoubtedly there will be some children who are capable of responding to music with expressive dance movements, which are self-initiated and teachers should plan their lessons so that these children can have an outlet for the manifestation of this artistic form. At the same time, however, many children are not able to dance in this way and unless teachers provide a learning framework of guided activities for them, there is every chance that they will feel uncomfortable, perhaps causing an opposite learning outcome from the one intended. The aesthetic development of all these children, gifted or otherwise, is paramount in a teacher's planning. At this age, then, dance lessons should be structured so that each child can succeed at his/her own level. This does not mean that the quality of output will be poorer, but that there will be variation in achievement. If the lessons are structured so that children can respond in their own way then this will be possible.

An acceptable format for the structure of dance lessons is that suggested in National Curriculum literature, i.e., a warm-up, followed by skill learning, culminating with a dance and concluded by a cool down activity. A suggested lesson might proceed as follows.

The warm-up can be a body awareness activity. An example of this would be to ask the children to listen to the sound of a tambourine being played and then ask them to move different parts of their body in response to the sound. A sequence might be: hands (from the wrists); arms (from the shoulders); feet (from the ankle); and legs (from the hip). The teacher should guide these actions so that all the children develop a repertoire and then give all of them the opportunity to choose which part of their bodies to move as the tambourine is played. Teachers should also awaken the children's kinesthetic awareness by asking the children to move slowly, or quickly, or lightly or with strength.

After this introductory warm-up stage, the children can then be taught some of the skills which they will also be learning in games and gymnastics but, in this instance, with a sound accompaniment. For example, they can be taught the skills of walking and skipping to music to the tune of 'Nellie the elephant' or to the music from the milk bottle TV advertisement ('The grasshopper's dance' by Bucalossi and J. Hylton). A good way to proceed would be for the teacher to give the children a demonstration of how to walk with a good posture and ask them to maintain a similar posture when they skip. Quality of stature is important in strengthening muscles and in developing poise.The children should also be expected to stretch their feet and point their toes towards the ground as they lift their knees on each skipping step. After giving the teaching guidance and using whichever piece of music is appropriate, let the children choose to dance freely to it so that those children who are capable can extend their movements. A teacher might expect to see these children skipping around on the spot, or skipping backwards or linking hands and skipping with a friend, whilst those who are not yet comfortable with this medium would practise what they had just been taught. The dancing part of a lesson structured in this way could then be a 'Follow the teacher dance'. Here, the teacher would line the children up so that each child was standing behind another and then would skip around the room with the line following. The teacher could skip in a curved pathway which travelled across the room from side to side in a snake-like formation, followed by skipping around the perimeter of the room until a circle is formed. The children could then all face into the centre of the circle and skip on the spot. Following all this activity, the cool-down should be quiet and calming. Teachers can use their voices very effectively at this stage. The children could be asked to find a 'magic spot' to stand on and then, as the teacher said the word s–t–r–e–t–c–h they could stretch high into the air and tense their bodies to ensure that every muscle was working to maintain body balance.

Much valuable language learning can take place through dance activities. Initially this learning will be connected with the naming of resources, e.g., 'drum', 'cymbal', 'tape-recorder' and so on. Children will also begin to understand some of the directional concepts which will be explored in dance activities, for example, 'right', 'left', 'around', 'straight', 'high', 'low', 'forwards', 'backwards', etc. It is also in dance activities where children combine verbal and motor responses as they respond to requests to move 'smoothly', or with 'spiky' arm shapes, or to dance with 'strong' or 'light' steps.

Altogether there are seven stages which children will move through before they can be fully operational in dance lessons. These are summarised below and could form effective principles for programmes to be based on during the early stages of dance teaching.

Space orientation

- Finding a space;
- moving in different ways to a space;
- stopping on command.

Naming the actions, and locomotor skills

- Walk, skip, etc.;
- small, big, short, tall;
- quickly, slowly, fast, faster, etc.

Identifying parts of the body

- Fingers, arms, feet, legs;
- shoulders, wrists, elbows, ankles, knees;
- hips, waist, tums, and bums;
- heels, tip-toes.

Naming the shape of the body

- Curled, stretched, twisted, bent.

Naming the objects and using them

- Drum, tambourine, maracas, bells, castanets, etc.

Positional language

- High, low, out, in;
- forwards, backwards, sideways;
- right, left, around;
- stand still, balance, behind, in front, at the side, one behind the other, in a line, in a circle, face, opposite.

Descriptive language

- Sink, spiky, smooth, strong, soft, light, heavy, quietly, stamp, slither, wobble, trot, explode.

As the year progresses, teachers should vary their approach to dance by choosing different stimuli, sometimes offering the children taped music, sometimes percussion, sometimes voice sounds, sometimes a story or a poem. They could also choose to develop the theme being explored in the classroom, or perhaps develop a specific dance skill, or link dance activity with a dramatic theme. There are many variations. Masks or Indian headdresses made in the art area of learning are useful stimuli for dramatic dancing, as are toys for use with 'Teddy Bears' Picnic', for example, or balloons, or scarves or ribbons. All these artefacts will give children an opportunity to develop their creative and aesthetic awareness and will help them to achieve the desirable learning outcomes concerned with development of the imagination, expression of their ideas, their listening skills, physical control, mobility and awareness of space.

GYMNASTIC ACTIVITIES

This aspect of learning is unique in the school curriculum, principally because the activities are solely connected with objective movement which allows children to use their bodies in a functional manner whilst at the same time helping them to develop important life skills. Most children like to climb on large apparatus, to balance walk along it and to jump down from it. Unfortunately when they first come to school, few of them have the skills to do this. So, after the introductory programme (see page 37) teachers should proceed slowly, taking the children through each new physical experience with some care. For instance, children should not be allowed to use the large apparatus until they have been taught some rudimentary gymnastic skills. It is important to remember that not all children will have had an opportunity to visit a children's playground before coming to school and there will be many who will not have chosen to play on climbing frames and slides during free choice play sessions in pre-school. Allowances must be made, too, for some children who will be disabled, whilst others may be overweight or clumsy. All children within such groups as these will not be physically capable of using the large apparatus and will certainly suffer negative experiences if they are expected to move about on surfaces which are high off the ground or which place physical demands on them beyond their kinaesthetic knowledge. They should all be taken through a structured programme which strengthens their arms and legs, which increases their flexibility, which develops their balance and co-ordination and which makes them skilled and proficient in bodily movement. It is very disconcerting to see many children in a fearful state when they are expected to balance walk across a plank which is a metre high from the floor before they have had any opportunity to practice controlling their body weight on the floor or at a lower level.

Generally, then, the aim of gymnastics lessons is to develop children's:

- natural abilities to run, jump, roll, climb and slide;
- mastery in balancing their bodies;
- ability to co-ordinate their motor movements;
- ability to control their body weight whilst moving;
- body strength.

The teaching method for gymnastics lessons will be very similar to the approaches to teaching used in the games lessons, i.e., the method will consist of open-ended tasks concerned with closed skills. For maximum benefit, the children will once again need some guided teaching followed by opportunities to experiment and practise the skills being taught. Guided teaching is an important feature of gymnastics teaching. A typical example of guided teaching taking place might be in a task suggestion such as 'jump up and down on two feet on the spot'. Here, in guiding the children to accomplish such a task, the teacher would focus on teaching the children the skill of controlling their body weight in the process of landing their bodies safely. The teacher would also highlight the factors which would allow this task to be accomplished, e.g., bending hips, knees and ankles as children put their body weight on the floor. Kinesthetic awareness could be developed by telling the children to feel as if they are sinking into the floor, or bouncing like a ball or landing lightly. Following this teaching input, the children should then be given opportunities to experiment with this new skill, perhaps by the teacher saying 'move about anywhere in the hall using light bouncy jumps'. Whilst the children are practising the teacher would then have the opportunity to help any children who might be having difficulty and also give alternative tasks to children who are physically disabled.

BUILDING UP A REPERTOIRE OF SKILLS

The skills which children need to learn and practise in the initial part of the curriculum are:

- transition of body weight from sitting to walking to running;
- transition of body weight from lying prone to lying supine;
- supporting body weight on different body parts, for example, left foot, lower back, right side, stomach;
- transition of body weight from one large body part to another, for example, bottoms and heels to prone position, lower legs to upper back;
- being able to stop in an upright forward movement, on a signal, with control;
- hopping and skipping;
- travelling on hands and feet keeping arms straight.

In building up a repertoire of skills, then, lesson formats should proceed in three stages, as follows:

- Stage 1: warm-up, skill learning, skill practice, cool-down;
- Stage 2: warm-up, skill learning, skill practice on benches, mats and low apparatus, cool-down;
- Stage 3: warm-up, skill practice on large apparatus, cool-down.

One of the skill learning topics listed below should be chosen by the teacher and the children should be taken through each type of lesson format in sequential order. Teachers will be able to assess when the children are ready to move on to each type of lesson. A general guide might be two lessons using the Stage 1 lesson format, two lessons using the Stage 2 format and four lessons using the Stage 3 format.

STAGE 1

Warm-up

Warm-up activities can be chosen from any of the following. Teachers should choose at least one from each group:

- walk, run, jump;
- circle arms, stretch arms high in the air, stretch arms wide;
- stretch fingers wide, clap hands, clench fists, wiggle fingers;
- stand on tip-toes, put body weight on heels, stamp feet;
- bend ankles, knees and hips, take a long step and hold the body position, touch knees and then toes;
- put hands flat on the floor and press down;
- walk and stop, run and stop;
- bend sideways, bend forwards, keep feet still and turn the upper body to face behind;
- circle wrists, shake hands vigorously;
- circle lower leg from knee whilst standing with feet shoulder-width apart, clap knees, sit on the floor and clap feet together, sit and clap knees together.

Skill learning and practice

If the skill of supporting body weight on different body parts was to be developed, for example, the activities could be centred around the following:

- standing on one foot;
- standing on tip-toes;
- putting body weight on bottoms only;
- putting body weight on lower legs, one lower leg, back, shoulders, one hand and one foot, two hands and two feet (make different shaped bridges), stomach, elbows and lower leg, head and knees.

After exploring all these different methods of supporting the weight of the body, the children could be guided to choose two different methods and to find a way of moving from one to the other.

Cool-down

Teachers can choose one or two of the following suggested activities to finish the lesson:

- walking with good posture;
- standing with arms and hands stretched high in the air or spread wide apart;
- sitting on the floor with a straight spine and stretched legs;
- lying supine with all body parts in a stretched position;
- lying supine, relaxed and with eyes closed;
- cross-legged sitting with a straight back;
- pointing to body parts when requested;
- following the teacher's action without a sound;
- following the teacher after being touched on the shoulder;
- walking backwards looking over shoulders;
- walking backwards with long strides;
- unfolding and stretching from a tucked position to a stretched position slowly and smoothly;
- copying the teacher's movements in silence.

STAGE 2

Warm-up

Warm-up activities should be taken from the list above.

Skill learning and practice

One of the skill learning activities should be developed, by using apparatus, e.g., mats, benches or low gymnastic activity tables. In the example being developed, 'the skill of taking weight on different parts of the body', the following activities should be covered.

Benches

- Travelling along the bench on feet, walking slowly, then quickly;
- travelling along the bench, stopping half-way along the bench and holding a position of stillness on two feet for three seconds before walking to the end of the bench;
- using different parts of the body to hold the body in stillness on the bench, lower leg, bottom, stomach, back, knees, each side of the body, one knee, one foot;
- using two parts of the body to hold the body in stillness: one hand and one foot, head and knee, elbow and knee, hands and knees, tip-toes;
- linking two, then three, still positions with linking movements.

Mats

- Hold positions of stillness on one foot, one knee, stomach, back, shoulders, bottom, head and feet, elbows and knees, each side of the body.

Table tops

- Climb up on to the flat surface and hold positions of stillness on bottom, lower legs, hands and feet, one hand and one foot, back, stomach, two feet.

Cool-down

The lesson should be finished with one or two of the cooling-down activities suggested earlier (see p. 50).

STAGE 3

Warm-up

Warm-up activities should be taken from the same activities which were used in both the Stage 1 and the Stage 2 lesson formats, but teachers will need to be aware that in these lessons the children will be using large apparatus and will need more strength to complete their skills. Consequently, emphasis should be placed on arm-warming activities in the general body-warming process.

Using large apparatus

The apparatus selected for supporting body weight on different body parts should enable the children to hold positions of stillness. The teacher should remind the children about the skill learning activities which they have been practising in earlier lessons and then organise the children into groups to work on the apparatus which has been chosen. Wherever possible groups should consist of no more than five children, so that the children can be active for most of the time. In the first apparatus lesson, the initial pre-requisite should be that the children are allowed to become familiar with it. In the second and subsequent lessons, the children should be guided to practise the skills which they have learned in earlier lessons. At all times, they should be encouraged to produce quality work which would consist of a good starting position, an interesting travelling movement to arrive at the position of stillness on the chosen part of the body, a good clear body shape held in stillness, followed by a good dismounting movement, concluding with a moment of stillness standing in an upright posture whilst standing on both feet.

Cool-down

The cool-down would follow and could consist of some of those activities already used.

ACQUIRING FURTHER SKILLS

When the children have acquired the skills listed above they will be ready to move on to new skill learning. As this development occurs, warm-up activities should now be changed to ensure that the children's bodies are ready for more complicated activities which will put more stress on their arms, legs and trunks.

For example, warm-up activities can be taken from the following groups:

- walking, running, skipping, hopping, jumping;
- walking on toes, heels and sides of feet, rolling the feet from heels along the sole of the foot to the toes and back again, shaking feet;
- shaking fingers, circling each finger in turn, moving fingers up and down quickly;
- lifting hands to touch shoulders and then straightening arms, stretching arms high above head and bending elbows so that the fingers touch upper back;
- moving shoulders up and down, circling shoulders, swinging arms out and bringing straight arms back to sides of body;
- bending neck so chin touches chest, stretching neck and letting head drop backwards;
- stretching and curling the whole body whilst standing and whilst lying down;
- lifting one knee high in the air, then the other, kneeling on the floor, keeping back straight, sit back on heels, then sit up again;
- pushing one hip outwards, then the other, pushing bottoms out, then stomachs, making a circular movement with the pelvis;
- walking and then holding the body in stillness on a signal, running and holding the body in stillness on a signal.

The new skill learning which children need to tackle now is as follows:

- identification and use of body parts;
- transference of body weight on, around and across intermediate equipment whilst in an upright position;
- travelling on hands and feet on, around, over, through and under intermediate equipment;

- stepping off low apparatus.

Possible ways of proceeding in each of these four areas are given below.

Identification and use of body parts

The action game called 'Simon says' is a fun method of identifying body parts.Teachers might like to try the following commands:

> Simon says: Put your elbows on the floor! Put two elbows on the floor! Hop on your left foot! Sit on your bottom! Spin around on your botttom! Lie on your back! Lie on your front! Lie on just your stomach! Wiggle your nose! Smile! Balance on one foot!

The next step would be to teach the children how to collect a piece of apparatus, e.g., a hoop, and place it ready for use. Teachers should use the hoops to create activities which reinforce the identification of body parts whilst, at the same time, developing the children's positional knowledge, for example:

- 'Hop around the hoop on your left foot!'
- 'Put your elbow inside the hoop!'
- 'Sit on your bottom inside the hoop!'
- 'Spin around on your bottom inside the hoop!'
- 'Kneel in your hoop!'
- 'Put your hands inside the hoop and your feet outside the hoop!'
- 'Put both your hands and your feet outside the hoop and make a bridge!'
- 'Jump into your hoop!'
- 'Run around the outside of your hoop on your toes!'
- 'Make a giant stride so that one foot is at one side of the hoop and one at the other!'
- 'Stand inside your hoop and stretch your fingers high in the air!'

To conclude the lesson, cool-down activities could be chosen from the following:

- children with a blue hoop could return their hoop and then sit on their bottoms with crossed legs;
- children with a green hoop could return their hoop and then lie down on their backs;
- children with yellow hoops could return theirs and stand on their feet;
- children with a red hoop could return theirs and kneel on their knees.

Another possible cool-down would be to suggest the following:

- 'Hold your hoop with two hands and put it high in the air.'
- 'Stand inside your hoop and stretch out wide.'
- Stand inside your hoop and lift it up around your waist, then over your head and carry it back to where you found it.'

Transference of body weight in an upright position

For this theme – after the warm-up – the children could practise the skills associated with locomotion, i.e., walking, running, skipping, hopping and jumping. Teachers should revise the skill of jumping with the children and should then teach the children how to skip, if they are not yet familiar with this skill. Teachers should also ensure that hopping and skipping are practised with good quality action. The children should be encouraged to keep their upper bodies erect as they move and should be guided to stretch their feet and point their toes towards the ground. Both movements should be practised with light bouncy steps and soft landings. The children can be expected to get out the hoops and place them as before. The locomotor skills can then be practised with each locomotor skill initially being practised freely. The children should be given an open-ended task such as, 'skip in the spaces between the hoops'. All the five locomotor skills should be practised in turn. Once again the teachers should ask for quality in the children's actions. The children should then be asked to use each of the five skills, in turn, to move around their own hoop. Teachers should help individual children to improve their performance as the children move around the hall.

In the lesson which follows this one, teachers should repeat these skill practices and then add the following new ones:

- ask the children to jump into their hoop and then jump out again;
- 'balance walk' around the hoop keeping as close to the hoop as possible;
- take a big walking step into the hoop and another one out again;
- hop into the hoop and out again;
- run around the hoop;
- run and jump over the hoop.

A change of apparatus would be appropriate for the next lesson, where teachers could teach children how to carry a gymnastic bench and place it safely. Many teachers are concerned that children of this age are not physically strong enough to complete this task and certainly if the benches are the adult size then these are genuine concerns. However, where benches are the proper size and weight for 3–7-year-old children, teachers can be assured that many children are quite capable of completing this activity. It also gives them a feeling of confidence, self-esteem and independence as they work on it, something which adds to their personal development.

To begin with, children should practise walking on the floor around the bench before being asked to walk along it. They should then take turns to walk slowly and carefully along the bench and step from it on to the floor. If the school does not have enough benches for the children to be active in groups of five, then half of the class could continue to practise activities such as jumping over the hoop or jumping or hopping into and out of the hoop, whilst the other half of the class use the benches. The most important factor at this stage in the gymnastics programme is to continue to develop the children's motor skills whilst at the same time giving them the confidence to carry, place and use apparatus.

Travelling on hands and feet, on, around, under, over and through

After the warm-up, the basis of this activity is that children should be shown how to move about on their hands and feet. Teachers should show the children how to crouch down, how to place their hands flat on the floor, shoulder-width apart, keeping their arms straight, and how to transfer their body weight from hand to hand and hand to foot, in a crawling action. The children should be encouraged to practise this skill and when they are ready should be encouraged to try to move backwards, sideways and around in a circle.

Hoops should be used to extend the children's knowledge of how to manage their body weight. The children should have guided experience in:

- crawling around the hoop, keeping as near to it as possible;
- crawling into and out of the hoop without touching it;
- crawling under a hoop held horizontally at knee-height by another child;
- crawling through a hoop held vertically by another child.

The lesson should finish with a cool-down. A stretching activity would be a good choice. The same lesson should be repeated, since the children will need time to develop their arm strength and their hand–foot co-ordination so that they will be confident when they start to use large apparatus.

The subsequent lesson should still be concerned with arm strength and co-ordination. After the warm-up, the children should be helped to understand the language which will be used in this lesson. The teacher should ask half the class to lie down whilst the other children should be asked to walk around the room stepping over the children who are lying down. Words such as across and from side to side should be used and explained. The children should then be asked to complete these actions whilst crawling on their hands and feet along the floor. One half of the class should then be asked to stand with their legs wide apart whilst the other half crawl through the space between their legs.

The apparatus used for the next part of the lesson can be gymnastic benches. To start with, the children should be reminded how to carry a bench and how to place it safely. Time should be spent on this skill since not only is it important in the management and organisation of gymnastics lessons, but it is also a life skill concerned with learning how to lift, carry and manoeuvre furniture. The children should be grouped so that there is maximum opportunity to be involved in action. They should then be guided through the following skill learning activities:

- crawling on hands and feet on the floor around the bench;
- crawling on hands and feet along the bench, and off the bench;
- crawling across the bench from side to side;
- crawling over the bench from side to side without touching it, if possible.

The cool-down session should be designed to give the children another opportunity to understand the language used in the lesson. For example, teachers can ask the children to lie on the floor and thread first one foot and then the other foot through clasped hands, or sit on the floor and poke a finger through the circle made with the thumb and finger of the other hand, or practise putting one leg over the other. They can be asked to stand with their hands under their feet (always good for a giggle!), to put their hands over their eyes, put their arms around their bodies or put their elbows on their feet.

Incidentally, in addition to being taught how to manoeuvre benches, children need to learn how to carry and place gymnastic mats, so that they can fulfil one of the general requirements for physical education in the National Curriculum, being taught 'how to lift, carry, place and use equipment safely' (Department for Education and Employment 1995: 2(3d)). Lifting, carrying and placing intermediate apparatus is a good precursor to using large apparatus in Key Stage 1.

An alternative to the 'Travelling' sequence using the mat might proceed as follows: After the warm-up the children can be taught how to work with others to learn the skill of mat management. This activity will help them to develop personal and social skills as well as mat management skills. Most children love the responsibility of being allowed to take part in this activity and teachers should not worry if children agitate for a turn or cry 'not fair!' if they are denied it!

There are many different sizes and weights of mats on the market and clearly teachers should use their common sense in deciding whether two children or four children should manage the mat. Once the mats are in place teachers should guide the children through several 'get-to-know-the-mat' activities such as asking them to try the following:

- walk around the mat, skip around the mat; run around the mat;
- stand on both feet in front of the mat and jump on to it, walk across it;
- hop on to the mat, hop across it, hop off it;
- jump on to the mat and use several jumps to cross it, step off it;
- stand with your back to the mat and walk backwards across it, and off it;

- walk across the mat, turn round and come back to where you started;
- crawl across the mat on your hands and feet only;
- crawl across the mat using your hands and lower legs only;
- roly poly across the mat;
- 'Can you move across the mat using your heels and bottoms?'
- 'Can you move across the mat using just your bottom?'
- 'You choose which of these activities you would like to do again.'
- 'Tell me if you think you know a new way to move across the mat.'

All these activities will ensure that every child has a wide experience of using the mat. Choice is built into the last two activities to allow those children who have confidence, ability and creativity to develop their emergent capabilities and yet provide a structure where every child can succeed. However, a cautionary note is perhaps needed at this point about the forward roll or somersault. Children of this age can rarely complete a forward roll or somersault properly. If they are allowed to try, they are invariably observed to be holding their spines straight rather than curling them. Doing a forward roll in this way causes jarring of the spine, is often part head stand and part a collapse in stability and balance, and is clearly not a forward roll. Fortunately, teachers have been lucky that not many serious accidents have ensued by allowing children to try this activity before their hands, arms and spines are strong enough to complete the task and so extreme care needs to be taken when children attempt it. A 'roly poly' roll or a tucked sideways roll will give the children just as much pleasure and also enough exercise and knowlege of turning and rolling at this stage in their development.

The cool-down following work with mats can be any calming activity. Some suggestions are:

- 'Lie on the floor, lift both legs and feet off the ground, and wiggle your fingers and toes.'
- 'Lie on the floor on your stomach and stretch your legs, arms, necks, fingers and toes.'
- 'Stand up with good posture and show me how to walk properly.'

Teachers might use the above activities for several lessons before moving on to the final skill of stepping off equipment.

Stepping off low apparatus

On the whole, most children will have had some experience of stepping off the benches earlier in this suggested programme but the importance of this activity may not have been emphasised. Now is the time to tackle it.

The warm-up prior to stepping off low apparatus can take any form. A suggestion might be to complete some foot activities such as:

- tapping one foot on the ground then the other;
- running around the area on tip-toes;
- stretching up high; stretching into a wide shape;
- taking long strides around the area;
- circling arms, wrists and ankles.

Then the skill learning part of the lesson should be concerned with balancing activities. Teachers might like to try the following:

- walk on toes, heels and sides of feet;
- walk forwards placing the heel of one foot in front of the toes of the other foot;
- stand on one leg and hold all parts of the body in stillness.

After these balancing activities the children should have the opportunity to focus on the skill of jumping. Teachers might like to ask the children to be involved in the following:

- hop on one leg, on the spot, change legs and hop on the other foot;
- hop anywhere you like in the hall;
- jump on two feet on the spot (focus on bending joints and soft landings);
- jump on two feet anywhere in the hall (focus on soft landings: 'be kind to your feet').

After these activities, teachers should then ask half the class to lie on the floor whilst the other half practise walking around the room stepping over the bodies. Activities can then be reversed. A development might be to ask the children to run around the hall in the spaces left between the bodies. All these activities will enable the children to balance their body weight in various situations, particularly on a forward momentum.

The children should then have another opportunity to get the benches into the required position before trying out the following:

- 'Step on to the bench, balance yourself, walk along the bench, step carefully off the end and walk back to your starting place'.
- 'Side-step along the bench from right to left, turn to face the end of the bench and step off'.
- 'Step on to the bench from the side, step off it, turn, step on, step off, turn, until you are at the end of the bench'.
- 'Walk along the bench and stand near the end on two feet, push off from two feet and land on the floor on two feet'.

Each of these activities should be practised many, many times before moving on to the next one. The third activity might be offered to the children as a choice if teachers have observed that some children are not confident with the two earlier tasks.

Finally, the cool-down activities can be chosen from the following:

- 'Put your weight on two flat hands and lift your bottom high in the air.'
- 'Try lifting one leg high and then the other'.
- Keep your feet still and try to move your hands a long way from your feet'.
- 'Sit with your legs crossed and your back straight'.

LARGE APPARATUS

When teachers observe that their children are confident in managing their bodies and managing small apparatus, then they can be introduced to activities on large apparatus. First of all, however, a word about the use of large apparatus.

Many of the problems associated with large apparatus are primarily to do with the space which the equipment occupies and also its size. The proper use of space is particularly important, especially as it relates to the teaching of gymnastic skills. As has been obvious throughout this chapter, the teaching of gymnastic skills is regarded as crucial for both the physical and personal well-being of children and needs to be attended to from a very early age. It is especially important for those children who are either fat, disabled or clumsy. All children need to be helped to cope with their physical selves and must have a structured programme if they are to succeed. As paediatric neurologist McKinlay (1988: 23) has observed: 'motor learning problems have been shown to be a persistent characteristic associated with educational failure, social isolation, anxiety withdrawal and depression persisting into adolescence.' All lessons connected with large apparatus must thus make some provision for teachers and children to pursue gymnastic skills, so, ideally, apparatus should not be erected before the children enter the school hall, which is the usual venue for large apparatus lessons. Easier said than done, most teachers would reply! How often does large apparatus work depend on circumstances which have nothing to do with children's physical development! Many schools – and teachers – however, have found effective solutions to the problems associated with equipment or with crowded school timetables which often restrict hall usage to 20 minutes for each class. Some schools, for example, take the apparatus out of storage areas before school starts and place it around the periphery of the hall so that teachers can put it out very quickly for their own class when the occasion arises. In other schools, the teacher and auxiliary often ask pre-school children to sit at one side of the hall whilst they erect climbing frames and some heavy equipment prior to the start of the lessson and then ask the children to help with mats or benches. In both these instances the emphasis is not only on flexibility but also on preserving both space and time for children to conduct their warm-up, skill practice and vigorous activity which is a necessary pre-requisite to apparatus work. The size of large apparatus, often seen as a hindrance to its use with small children need not necessarily be a handicap, although pre-schoolers should never be expected to erect apparatus which has been selected for use by older primary school children. Some schools, however, have overcome this problem by investing in nursery and Key Stage 1 equipment which is now available from most manufacturers (see resources section). Much of this equipment is both light and small enough for 4-year-old children to manage.

Whatever the problems associated with the use of large apparatus appear to be, it is important to try to overcome them in order to provide children with space. Since the suggested format for large apparatus lessons is very similar to that discussed earlier in connection with other physical activities i.e., warm-up, skill learning and cool-down, it is essential that opportunities for cardiovascular work are preserved. Much of what follows in relation to teaching, therefore, assumes that children will be given ample opportunity for activity both before and after their work on large apparatus.

In a typical large apparatus lesson then, and after suitable warm-up, the class could be divided up into two groups, giving each group a name, e.g., Suns and Moons, or Stars and Planets, so that the children can identify themselves when instructions are given. Each adult should be responsible for one group. Each group would then be expected to choose to use apparatus activities in their own half of the hall. The value of this is twofold – the children will be prevented from wandering around the hall avoiding the activities and the adult's attention, and the adult will have a better opportunity to observe, assess, guide and teach the children. After half of the time has elapsed, the children can exchange places and the adult will move with them into the other half of the hall.

Teachers should arrange the apparatus so that the children can practise the skills which they have already learned earlier in the programme. Mats and benches should be placed strategically so that the children can practise and improve these skills with plenty of time at their disposal. This will give some security to those children who are not yet feeling confident. The children should be allowed to explore all the equipment in their half of the hall freely. Each adult should observe each child and ensure that they are active. If children choose to climb they will invariably only climb to a height with which they are comfortable, so adults should have no concerns about this. However, they should not press the children to climb higher than this self-selected height. For some children, incidentally, this may mean that they only climb on to the first rung of the climbing frame. Praise and encouragement should be given readily for this kind of achievement, however, since the act of climbing is another important moving milestone and also an important life skill. In today's society children often have no other chance in their lives to learn to climb a ladder except when they use large apparatus at school. Children who climb up trees, for example, are often considered to be environmentally unfriendly, whilst those who climb on cars or railings will be thought of as embryo vandals! It is also the case that the number of children who can access this activity in a local authority playground is minimal. Yet in life we have to have the confidence to climb ladders to hang curtains, replace light bulbs, to decorate, to clean and to wash windows.

For all work on large apparatus, the advice to teachers is always to proceed slowly, so that the children can become very familiar with the apparatus and its properties. If they are allowed to choose both their apparatus and their activity they will soon be observed to be making progress. They will start to climb higher, and will undoubtedly increase their repertoire of activities on both the benches and the mats. Those children who are physically competent will become creative and try new movements which the adult can guide. Children with special needs will also grow in confidence in this free choice environment, but must be encouraged to practise the skills to which they have been introduced. If the children are statemented, their assistant should be able to guide them through a structured programme in this type of setting. Similarly, clumsy children should be guided by their adult, and those who are overweight should be observed carefully to ensure that they are active. Incidentally, free choice does not mean that the children should not be encouraged to try all the motor learning activities which are on offer. Over a number of weeks, the adults present should persuade each child to work with each piece of large apparatus and try the skills which apply to it.

Throughout the initial programme, the children's performance should be assessed by both adults and any assistants before the apparatus layout is changed. It is important for teachers to resist the temptation to put out equipment which the children are not capable of using to maximum benefit. Children of this age, for instance, are seldom ready to jump competently from high stools and boxes and can certainly not control their bodies effectively when landing from a height. Similarly, few children are ready to balance walk on the narrow side of gymnastic benches or on planks suspended at height.

Finally, it is important for teachers to be constantly reminding themselves that before the children are asked to try any new movement on large apparatus they should have an opportunity to practise the movement on the floor in the skill learning part of the lesson.

Throughout all the programmes which have been discussed in this chapter, whether they be concerned with gymnastics, games, dance or the use of apparatus, the four parameters of human development with which the teacher should be concerned are:

- motor activity which involves large movements and body postures which lead to physical competence and economy of effort;

- fine motor activity which will develop visual competence and associated manipulative skills;
- auditory competence in hearing and listening, and the use of language codes;
- social competence in organising self and acceptance of codes of conduct.

It is also worth re-stating at this point the desirable outcomes in the physical development area of learning (SCAA 1996: 4) which require that children should be developing control, mobility, awareness of space and manipulative skills in indoor and outdoor environments. The document also reminds teachers that children should be encouraged to form positive attitudes towards a healthy and active way of life.

Teachers often ask which motor skills children should be able to perform at the end of each school year and the following list of specific motor skills should assist teachers in making objective assessments of normative development in children reaching the end of their fourth year.

SPECIFIC PHYSICAL SKILLS WHICH SHOULD BE ACQUIRED AT THE END OF YEAR FOUR

And so, at the end of the fourth year, children should be able to complete the following tasks:

- walk on a narrow line;
- run lightly on toes;
- run a distance of 35 metres in 9.95 seconds;
- climb, slide and swing skilfully;
- skip on alternate feet;
- move rhythmically to music;
- stand on one foot for 8–10 seconds;
- grip strongly with either hand;
- hop on either foot on the spot;
- hop 3 metres forwards on either foot;
- bend and touch toes without flexing knees;
- send a large ball with feet (kick) or hands (roll) along a straight pathway;
- jump from two feet to two feet a distance of 77.83cms;
- throw a bean bag a distance of 496.5cms;
- undress and dress without assistance.

These skills should be achieved by all normal 4-year-old children. Some children will be capable of reaching higher-order skills and will demonstrate their competence, which should be recorded. Some will not reach the normative level and these children should be carefully monitored and any motor deficiencies should be attended to through special programmes.

The chapters which follow will be concerned with the teaching and learning of Physical Education in the statutory age of schooling and will look at building on the skill framework suggested here.

Chapter 4

Gymnastic activities in Key Stage 1

This chapter is intended to build on the information on gymnastic activities which was presented in Chapter 3. Together they form both a horizontal and a vertical curriculum of gymnastic activities for children who are in the first stage of statutory schooling. The information in both chapters is built on knowledge about the developmental stages which normal children move through as they grow and develop their physical selves.

As was indicated previously, gymnastic activities are concerned almost entirely with objective movements which allow children in this age group to use their bodies in a functional manner to develop important life skills. The National Curriculum Working Group, in its Interim Report (1991: 76) tells us that:

> Gymnastic activities focus on the body. They are concerned with acquiring control, co-ordination and versatility in the use of the body, and responding to challenges. They are based on natural actions such as leaping, balancing, inverting, rolling and swinging.

Other authorities would appear to take a similar view. Heath *et al*. (1994), for instance, suggest that the focus in gymnastic activities is entirely on the body and that this medium offers opportunities for physical activity and learning which differ from other areas of the Physical Education curriculum. They suggest that children can develop their potential for exploration through natural movement if they are challenged and guided in a safe but stimulating environment. Davies and Sabin (1995) also believe that movement is a medium through which children can learn about themselves and express their feelings. They also suggest that gymnastics is mainly concerned with the development of skilful body management and describe it as 'objective in purpose' (p. 1). Another view is expressed by Smith, in Bunker, Hardy, Smith and Almond (1994), who, whilst agreeing that gymnastic activities offer exciting and challenging experiences for children, shows some concern for those teachers who may not have received adequate training and who might pass on their lack of confidence and subsequent anxieties to their children. The result, argues Smith, could be that gymnastics offers a threat to children and not a challenge.

Manners and Carroll (1991), however, would dispute such a view. They are confident that early years teachers in the main show both an understanding of the nature of early years education and have extensive knowledge about child development. It is likely, too, that early years teachers understand the importance of the provision of what Manners and Carroll call a 'gymnastics environment' (pp. 1–2) in which children can progress at their own rate, from moving instinctively and hesitantly to performing competently, with understanding and awareness. Manners and Carroll also believe that natural actions, which I would call the moving milestones in the continuum of physical development and skill acquisition, form the basis of movement education which in turn leads to gymnastics.

In terms of the statutory requirements for the gymnastic activities area of the curriculum at this stage, one need look no further than the National Curriculum for Physical Education (Department for Education and Employment 1995: 3(2a, b)) Key Stage 1 Programme of Study which states that:

Pupils should be taught:

  a different ways of performing the basic actions of travelling using hands and feet, turning, rolling, jumping, balancing, swinging and climbing both on the floor and using apparatus;
  b to link a series of actions both on the floor and using apparatus, and how to repeat them.

It is also interesting to note here that the National Curriculum in Physical Education also has a list of statutory General Requirements which pupils are expected to acquire across the age range from 5 to 16. These General Requirements, which permeate all the areas of activity in all programmes of study at each of the four key stages are grouped into three specific areas:

1. the promotion of physical activity and healthy lifestyles . . .
2. the development of positive attitudes . . .
3. the necessity to ensure safe practice.

(Department for Education and Employment 1995: 2)

The National Curriculum documentation also says that 'Physical education should involve pupils in the continuous process of planning, performing and evaluating' although the greatest emphasis, it is stated, should be on 'the actual performance aspect of the subject' (*ibid.*). These general requirements then apply to the teaching of Physical Education across all key stages, and must be considered along with the requirements for the gymnastic activities area of the Physical Education curriculum.

Part of the previous chapter was concerned with introducing children to gymnastic activities before statutory schooling. The basis for this programme was the suggestions in earlier chapters which were concerned with the development of physical skills or movement milestones, first, during babyhood, for example, rolling, crawling and climbing, and second, during the toddler stage, for example, walking, running, climbing, hopping, turning and rolling. During this pre-school period, children are mastering their ability to balance their bodies in various static and dynamic situations, developing their co-ordination and visual perception, increasing their strength and always finding out, by trial and error, what their bodies can and cannot do.

Children who have attended a pre-school are almost certain to have been introduced to the physical development area of learning, one of the six areas of learning which form the curriculum in pre-schools. Those children who have not had these experiences, however, should be given the opportunity to follow the gymnastic activities programme outlined in the previous chapter. Once this has been done, the physical competencies achieved by each child should be recorded so that Key Stage 1 teachers will know which developmental level each child has reached. This assessment procedure will be particularly valuable in relation to those children classified as having special needs, an area which needs defining in relation to gymnastic activities.

At this stage, there could be many different types of special need which children present to teachers. The most obvious one is where children are statemented and need the support of another adult when taking part in Physical Education lessons. For the purpose of indentification and assessment, a useful document for teachers to use here would be the *Code of Practice on the Identification and Assessment of Special Educational Needs* (Department for Education 1994) which, among other things, contains support programmes specially prepared for statemented children. There are other children, of course, with milder forms of special education needs (SEN) conditions, many of which teachers have been aware of for years. Conditions such as asthma, cystic fibrosis, diabetes, cardiac conditions and epilepsy have been in mainstream education for a long time and most teachers know how to ensure a safe environment for children who suffer from such conditions. Other 'special conditions' would include children who have slight hearing or slight visual and spatial problems which affect their balance or co-ordination, or their visual and spatial perception. A particularly difficult group to deal with could be those children who have problems which have not been specifically identified. The most obvious in this group could be those children who, in the past, have been termed 'clumsy', and who will need constant assistance, not only to complete the gross and motor skills demanded in many gymnastic tasks, but also the fine motor skills tasks required of them in the classroom. It is interesting to note that two researchers, Sugden and Wright (1996), consider the term 'clumsy' to have derogatory connotations, preferring to call the condition as it exists in children a Development Co-ordination Disorder (DCD). Sugden and Wright argue children with DCD can acquire the basic motor skills but their acquisition may be delayed, and the children may have difficulty in using them flexibly to adapt to changing environmental demands. Initially, however, these children often look awkward, so Key Stage 1 teachers can be helpful in identifying the condition in gymnastic activities where the functional aspects of movement can be readily observed. Finally, a special plea for those children who have achieved a high level of competence, so much so in fact that in other subject areas they could be classified as 'gifted'. It is very easy to neglect them at the expense of others because of the fact that they are regarded as competent. Whilst they may not be children with 'special needs' in the usual sense of the phrase, they may need special attention!

Taking into account the needs of all children then, the ability of teachers to offer a gymnastic environment where all children can make progress is of crucial importance and the ultimate challenge. Clearly the success of building such an environment will depend on the methods which teachers choose to use in delivering the National Curriculum so that children reach the End of the Key Stage in Physical Education satisfactorily, and happily. As one might expect, questions of 'methodology' are thought-provoking. The School Curriculum Assessment Authority (SCAA) and the Curriculum Assessment Authority of Wales (ACAC), in their Guide to the National Curriculum, are quite clear about what should happen:

> It is for schools to decide how and to what depth to teach material contained in the programmes of study. No methodology is implied; it is a matter for teachers' professional judgment to decide the most effective and efficient way of teaching the National Curriculum.
>
> (ACAC and SCAA 1996: 9)

They also state that teachers can decide whether to include material from outside a Programme of Study in order to develop the school curriculum.

It appears then that it is up to schools and teachers to decide what to do, and if this proves to be the case – as one expects it will – then one has to speculate on how it might be accomplished. In the main, the methods which teachers have been persuaded to use in the past have been influenced by research. In this connection, two important 'models' may have been, first, Tanner (1978) whose research showed the wide variation in the growth patterns of each child, the implications of which would suggest that didactic whole class teaching methods would not be useful if all children were to progress at their own rate of learning and, second, Blenkin and Kelly (1987), who, amongst others, postulated the theory that the different inherited and environmental differences in which children have been nurtured suggest the importance of presenting teaching subjects within a frame of a permissive environment. These 'models' are neatly summed up by Jones (1996) who concludes that methods which focus on child-centred learning, which accommodate individual differences, which enable the implementation of a structure of provision and which allow for differentiation in both task and solution, are those which have been most favoured.

If this is true, then teachers have been persuaded to use an 'open-ended' or 'process' model of learning, whereby children are set tasks which they can fulfil according to their own level of ability. In terms of Physical Education, sometimes the task given will be 'constrained' – for instance, the teacher might ask the children to skip and stop, whilst, at other times, the teacher using the open-ended method might ask the children to choose their own way to travel along a bench on their hands and feet, which will not only give the children an opportunity to work at their own level, but will also give the teacher an opportunity to give teaching assistance to individual children. By using this method the children can reach their own individual potential and be encouraged to perform their own response to the given task with good quality movements.

Whatever methodology is used to teach children or to create a 'child-friendly' environment, however, the safety of children during physical activities is extremely important. In this regard, the book *Safe Practice in Physical Education* (BAALPE 1995) is a text which all those who work in Physical Education should consult on matters of safety. Every aspect of safety is covered, including PE and the law, qualifications and supervision, the curriculum and extra-curricular activities, risk assessment, management and administration, clothing, personal effects and protection, pupils with special needs, accidents, first aid and HIV/Aids, insurance, environment and equipment.

Specifically, and to address the fundamental safety points in relation to gymnastic activities:

- the children must be managed satisfactorily;
- each task set should be suitable for the age and abilities of the children;
- all progressive steps in learning an activity should be included and each step should be thoroughly consolidated before moving on to the next (this is particularly important for children with disabling conditions);
- there should be enough space to complete the task;
- the apparatus should be the correct size and weight for the children 'to lift, carry, place and use . . . safely';
- climbing apparatus should be the correct height for the children who are using it;
- children should be taught 'about the safety risks of wearing inappropriate clothing, footwear and jewellery';

- children should be made aware of the importance of warming up before and cooling down after exercise.

The General Requirements for Physical Education in all key stages are explicit in stating the importance of safe practice and of teaching pupils about 'the importance of responding readily to instructions and recognising and following relevant rules, etiquette and safety procedures for different activities' (Department for Education and Employment 1995: 9).

Moving on from theoretical to more practical matters, the next stage would be to organise the gymnastic activities programme. The programme for Key Stage 1 children should be part of a whole school policy which considers the content and philosophy of the Physical Education curriculum for all the children in any school. Since continuity is essential, the Key Stage 1 gymnastic activities programme should be formulated with the pre-school teachers so that progression can be achieved, and with Key Stage 2 teachers so that gifted children can progress through the key stage where necessary. ACAC and SCAA (1996) suggest that teachers should consider the following points when planning a Programme of Study:

- ways in which different sections of the programme of study inter-relate;
- what pupils were taught in the corresponding section of the programme of study at the previous stage and what they will be taught in the next key stage;
- how to revisit some aspects of the programme of study to consolidate earlier work;
- how to ensure there are sufficient opportunities for differentiated work for pupils of all abilities.

(ACAC and SCAA 1996: 9)

Once the Programme of Study and the gymnastic area of activity has been agreed, a scheme of work should then be constructed with input from the whole staff. In this scheme, there should be appropriate content for each age group and differentiated content for children with special needs. It should be planned around the framework of the National Curriculum but geared up to local circumstances and requirements.

To get teachers started, there are many schemes of work which have been specially prepared by Physical Education specialists. Some of these have been prepared as LEA schemes, whilst others have been published for the commercial market. Almost all of them are useful to teachers who might be searching for guidance in the construction of a scheme of work for Key Stage 1 gymnastic activities. Nevertheless, it is essential that all the staff in a school decide together which of these schemes they will use so that continuity and progression across the age range is not jeopardised.

Some published schemes of work, incidentally, are structured on a lesson-by-lesson approach, whilst others provide frameworks of ideas which staff can use as a foundation on which to form their own structure for their own particular circumstances. Whichever scheme is chosen, the most important factors for teachers to consider are whether:

- the scheme is suitable for the age and developmental stage of their own children;
- it is possible to differentiate the gymnastic tasks which are suggested in the scheme;
- the scheme is progressive enough to allow the children to develop physically;
- the scheme promotes physical activity and healthy lifestyles;
- the scheme promotes positive attitudes;
- the scheme ensures safe practice.

The scheme of work should also contain details of the gymnastic themes to be explored in each year, and which should be revisited from the preceding year. Units of work should be agreed and the content should be outlined.

The contents of proposed schemes of work for gymnastic activities based on the gymnastic skills which children need to learn in Year 1 and Year 2 now follow. Both years are treated separately.

GYMNASTIC ACTIVITIES FOR YEAR 1

The gymnastic skills which children need to learn in Year 1 are the following:

- holding the body still on different body parts;
- hopping and skipping;
- rocking and rolling;
- travelling on hands and feet;
- travelling on different body parts;
- stretching and curling the body.

These skills can be covered as six gymnastic 'themes' set out as above in the order in which they are listed. The themes are suggested in this order to accommodate the physical growth and development stages which normal children will be moving through in their fifth year, and their first year of statutory schooling.

Teachers are advised that if children are going to acquire the skills within the scheme satisfactorily and with confidence, then each theme should be developed by giving children activities and skill tasks which involve work on the floor first, before asking them to solve skill tasks connected with the theme on apparatus.This procedure is particularly important for children with disabling conditions. During the first few lessons, therefore, the children should not use the large apparatus. The format of lessons should be identical to the formats suggested in the last chapter, i.e., a warm-up, followed by the introduction to and practising of various skills, concluding with a cool-down. The first lessons will follow this suggested pattern while the next lessons will begin with a warm-up, will revisit some of the skills already learned and will then be consolidated by allowing the children to practise their skills on low-level equipment. Finally the last lessons in a theme series will consist of a warm-up, a reminder about the skills which have been learned and then skill practice on the large apparatus.

Before looking in detail at suggestions for working within the gymnastic themes, a word about warm-up activities. Before children start to take part in gymnastic activities it is very important for teachers to provide a suitable warm-up. This should consist of vigorous activities, with particular attention being given to the stretching of the major muscle groups and cardiovascular preparation.

Warm-up ideas for Year 1

Before moving on to some new activities, teachers can revisit the warm-up ideas suggested for the 4-year-olds in the last chapter, or develop some of the action rhymes which were suggested for the nursery children. The most suitable action rhymes to revisit and develop are the following:

- 'Here we go round the mulberry bush' (skip in the circle to build up cardiovascular circulation);
- 'Heads and shoulders, knees and toes' (keep spines straight when touching toes and double the speed of delivery to increase motor co-ordination and cardiovascular functioning);
- 'Knees up Mother Brown' (cardiovascular functioning, motor skill practice and fun!)
- 'One finger, one thumb, keep moving' (increase the pace and ensure that the children really warm-up their fingers by telling them to stretch each digit);
- 'Peter taps with one hammer' (double the speed of delivery to increase the mobility of the joints and to put mild stress on the muscles).

The following ideas may also be useful.

Circles (joint flexibility, stretching muscle groups, concept of 'circle')

- Walking and jogging in a circle, controlled stop;
- circling fingers, wrists, arms, ankles, knees, hips, turning on the spot;
- stretching high to make circles with fingers above heads;
- stretch arms wide and make a circle with fingers;

- reach out to make a circle on the floor with each foot in turn;
- use one finger to trace the largest imaginary circle possible in front of the body, then at each side of the body.

Walking (muscle tone of the spine, stretching the large muscle groups, understanding quality and speed of movements)

- Re-visit the ideas outlined in 'Stage 2' in Chapter 3;
- walk with good posture: holding arms high in the air and stretching, on tip-toes, with arms stretched wide, backwards, side steps, turning on the spot, giant strides, with knees up high, walking slowly then quickly, walking heavily then lightly, penguin steps;
- play starships (wide arms), battleships (two arms together pointing forward) and galactic missiles (turning around and around with arms held high in the air)

Running (cardiovascular functioning, joint flexibility)

- Forwards, stop with control; running around 'magic spots' placed on the ground; run and when asked, touch the floor with a hand and stop in a crouched position.

Change

- From jogging to running to walking to jogging to running and so on.

Stretch

- Wide shape;
- long shape;
- arms only;
- whole body;
- lying down then standing up.

Jack-in-the-box

- Crouch down, jump up and stretch.
- 'Jack-in-the-box, will he come out? Yes he will!'

Crawling

- On hands and feet;
- forwards;
- backwards;

- sideways;
- around in a circle.

'Bean game'

- Jelly bean (wobble all body parts);
- jumping bean (jump from place to place);
- frozen bean (stand still on the spot);
- runner bean (run around the space);
- chilli bean (hop from one foot to the other);
- French bean (do the high kicking step which is characteristic of the can-can);
- baked bean (lie down on the floor with arms wide, as if lying in the sun).

Happy song

- 'If you're happy and you know it': clap your hands, stamp your feet, pat your head, touch your feet, bend your knees, shake your feet, shrug your shoulders and so on.

'Body parts game'

- Run, and on a signal, touch the floor with the body part which the teacher calls out.

Teachers should make sure that the children really are stretching during all the stretching activities. A good method to use to check this is to look carefully at the children's faces, as those who are really stretching will have contorted faces! Simply doing the actions does not necessarily mean that the children are warming up their bodies – it's the quality of the effort which will produce the desired results. Teachers should also make sure that proper cardiovascular preparation is being achieved by observing whether the children are huffing and puffing. If children are really working hard they will not have enough spare breathing capacity to talk or to comment on the actions. This is a good time to teach the children 'about the changes which occur in their bodies as they exercise, and to recognise the short-term effects of exercise on their bodies' (Department for Education and Employment 1995: 3). And so on to suggestions for tackling the gymnastic themes.

Holding the body still on different body parts

This theme is intended to help focus the children's attention on the parts of their body which they can hold still. The body has broad surfaces such as the back, stomach, bottom, hips and shoulders, which can be used to support its weight. Less broad surfaces such as the shins and smaller areas such as knees and hands can also be used to support the body; when using these areas it is much harder to keep the body still.

The aim in exploring this theme is to develop the children's ability to control their body weight when holding themselves on different surfaces of their body, and also to become more aware of the ease or the difficulty of supporting parts of the body in various circumstances. It is particularly useful to use at the beginning of the school year when children may have experienced a growth spurt during the summer months.

Floorwork activities

After the warm-up, the children can try various weight-bearing activities, so that they become aware of the concept of stillness.

The activities are listed in order of difficulty. Ask the children to:

1 Walk about the area and stand absolutely still when the command 'freeze' is given. After many practices, let the children practise stopping suddenly and standing still after running at speed. Children with DCD might find this task difficult and could cover up their apparent inability by 'clowning' around. Teachers should take note and watch for other symptoms. Children in wheelchairs and children with other disabling conditions should be encouraged to take part and do the best they can. Children who are gifted should be expected to 'freeze' more quickly in response to the command and hold the position of stillness for longer.

2 Lie down on their backs and stay absolutely still. Children in wheelchairs can sit absolutely still, with their hands touching their backs.

3 Lie on the front of their bodies and hold a position of stillness. Gifted children can be expected to hold a stretched body position. Immobile children should put both hands on their chest with their elbows high.

4 Lie first on the left side of their bodies and then the right side of their bodies. Again, gifted children should be expected to hold a good stretched body position. Children in wheelchairs should be asked to sit still with first their left arm held high, then their right arm held high.

5 Lift their legs and arms off the floor and hold all body parts still. Children in wheelchairs should lift any mobile limbs into a space. Gifted children should be encouraged to stretch their limbs as far as possible.

6 Stand on tip-toes and hold a position of stillness. Other options: push down on to a surface and try and straighten arms, move body weight on to one part of bottom.

7 Choose which part of their body they would like to put their weight on and hold a position of stillness, then another and another.

8 Hold a position of stillness on their bottoms only. Encourage all the children to tense their muscles, (and tell them why this helps them to

balance). Allow some children to support themselves with two hands, some with one and insist on the gifted completing the task with no support from their hands.

9 Walk, then run, and on the command 'freeze' stop with both legs in an astride position.

10 Walk, then run, and 'freeze' in any shape the children choose – no wobbling! Children in wheelchairs should wave their arms in the air and complete as much upper body movement as possible.

11 Lie on the fronts of their bodies and lift their legs, their arms and their upper bodies off the floor. Encourage the gifted children to hold a position of stillness on the smallest part of their torso possible. They could try to touch their heads with their feet and hold a position of stillness.

12 Hold a position of stillness whilst the weight is on two lower legs and then one lower leg. Wheelchair children and gifted children could be asked to spread their arms in a crucifix position.

Teachers can choose a few of the above ideas and then might like to introduce some equipment such as mats, magic spots, planks and EDRA logs, cubes or cylinders (see Resources) to give children another dimension when learning to understand the concept of holding their body in stillness. These can be chosen by the children and set out by them. Teachers can then ask the children which positions of stillness they are proposing to practise on the equipment they have chosen and can then move around the environment helping individual children to develop good quality body shapes as they hold these positions.

In later lessons, when the children are deemed to be competent, they can be introduced to larger apparatus (see Chapter 3 for detailed discussion on the use of large apparatus). Teachers can decide whether to involve the children in the planning of the layout, but the children 'should lift, carry and place the apparatus' (Department for Education and Employment 1995: 2), ready for action. Teachers should set open-ended apparatus tasks such as 'Explore your apparatus'. (This is an important function which is not theme-focused so that the children can become familiar with the apparatus, before the teacher sets skill tasks. This option should always be offered when a new apparatus layout is in use.)

After this, a new task may be suggested each week, for example:

- 'Choose a place on your apparatus where you can hold a position of stillness.'
- 'Choose one part of your body on which to hold a position of stillness and show me two places on your apparatus where you can do this.'
- 'Show me all the places on the apparatus where you can hold your position of stillness.'
- 'Show me a different part of your body on which you can hold a position of stillness.'

- 'Steer your wheelchair around the obstacles and show me how you can hold it in a position of stillness.Now show me how you can stop on the magic spots. Now how to steer between the spots and stop still when asked, showing me a stretched body shape.'

Teachers should encourage the children to plan, practise and refine their movements on the apparatus. They should also encourage them to link their positions of stillness with actions which take them from one to the other so that they make a movement pattern which they can remember and will be able to perform if asked. This particular theme will give teachers an excellent opportunity to encourage children to stand absolutely still with good posture before starting their movement pattern, and to stand still with good posture on completion.

The large apparatus might involve children in practising skills which it is not possible to practise either on the floor or on low-level equipment, for example, holding themselves in stillness on the climbing frame. Initially, children working on the frame should be guided by the teacher so that they have some ideas of possible skills to practise. They can then choose their own in response to open-ended task suggestions made by the teacher. Some children may choose to sit happily on the rungs of the climbing frame and hold a good body shape in responding to the task suggestion, whilst others can be expected to hang from their knees or their hands.The gifted will be able to practise the skill which they learned on the floor, balancing on their bottoms without using their hands or legs to support their body weight, whilst holding a good body position.

The culmination of work on any theme should result in each child showing a movement pattern which contains elements of his/her ability to hold the body in stillness whilst maintaining a good body shape, on areas of their bodies on which they have chosen to perform. Children should always be encouraged to perform their movement patterns for their peers and praise should be given for good quality of performance, rather than for the difficulty of task selected.

Cool-down ideas

- Walk with good posture;
- lie in a supine position and pull each leg in turn on to chest;
- lie in a prone position and lift head and chest off the floor.

Hopping and skipping

This theme could be a general theme which is taught across all three areas of activity in each lesson for a concentrated period of perhaps two or three weeks. Paediatric literature suggests that children can skip by the time they are 4 years old and that whilst the ability to hop is a skill which emerges later, it should be possible to acquire it no later than the fifth year. Consequently then, these two fundamental skills can be experienced in dance and games lessons at the same time they are introduced in gymnastics lessons.

For this theme, and after the warm-up, teachers might like to ask the children to try the following activities:

- jumping on two feet on the spot, then moving freely around the area;
- walking freely around the area with each knee lifted high on each step;
- step forward on one foot and hold a position of stillness; then the other foot;
- step forward on one foot and hold a position of stillness with the other foot held off the floor;
- then with the knee held high;
- stand on one foot, keep the other foot off the ground, and hop on the chosen foot;
- hop freely around the area; keep changing feet;
- use hopping to move from one end of the area to the other;
- step on the left foot, keeping the right foot off the ground, then hop on the left foot; keep the right foot off the ground for a moment, then step forward with the right foot, place it on the ground, lift the left foot up, keep it in the air and hop on the right foot; keep the left foot in the air for a moment, then step forward on to the left foot; and so on until the children are skipping;
- children in wheelchairs should be asked to use their hands to tap on the arms of their wheelchair for all these activities. They should be able to pick up both the hopping rhythm and the skipping rhythm with their hands. Ask the children to exaggerate their movements so that they stretch their upper bodies and gain maximum exercise.

All the children should be shown how to complete the two skills of hopping and skipping in each lesson, and this should be followed by activities where they can use these skills. Teachers might like to try the following.

Ropes

- Use one foot to hop over the rope many times;
- hop on one foot forwards, alongside and parallel to the rope;
- hop over the rope on one foot then turn and hop over it to return to the starting position;
- skip alongside the rope.

Hoops

- Hop into the hoop on one leg and hop out on the same leg;
- hop into the hoop, turn, and hop back to starting position;
- skip around the hoop;
- skip around the area in between the hoops;
- skip around any hoop in the area;
- skip in the spaces around the hoops, on the command 'hop', step into a hoop and hop on one leg.

EDRA spots

- Hop on to a spot, hop off the spot, hop over the spot;
- step on to the spot and hop on it;
- hop on one foot from one spot to another;
- hop on to a spot and turn around whilst hopping;
- skip around the spot;
- skip in and out of all the spots.

Because these activities place stress on the feet, legs and the hips, as well as on leg and foot joints, teachers should consider an 'opposing' activity to provide a contrast to the learning of the two skills, for example:

- 'Lie on the floor on your backs (then fronts) and make yourself as long as possible.'
- 'Lie on your side and stretch out as far as you can. Can you make a banana shape?'
- 'Lie on the floor – you choose in which position – and make yourself floppy.'
- 'Put both hands flat on the floor, keep your arms straight, and kick your legs in the air.'
- 'Sit on your bottom and spin around on the floor.'

Children in wheelchairs should be allowed to wheel along the ropes and around the hoops and the spots. Teachers can decide if they need their own special area or whether they can be active with the other children. They should certainly join in the 'opposing' activities, stretching and being floppy in their wheelchairs! They might like to spin around on their wheelchairs! – or be encouraged to practise turning movements around their spine to increase their upper body mobility.

Cool-down ideas

- Walk with long strides, keeping spine straight;
- standing on the spot, stretch into one long stride and hold the position;
- stand on tip-toes and hold the position.

Rocking and rolling

Rolling is an essential skill in gymnastics because it is a useful linking movement at all developmental stages – even Olympic gymnasts need to know how to roll! In addition, many advanced skills in gymnastics depend on an ability to rotate the body on to, around, over, along and off pieces of equipment and to rotate in the air and along the floor. Rocking is a helpful pre-activity leading into rolling, and enables children to gain confidence in transferring their weight from one part of the body to another. Wherever they are rolling or pre-rolling children should work on mats so that they develop more confidence. Also, a variety of movement tasks should be presented so that they can discover just how the surfaces and parts of their bodies can be used. Incidentally, this is a very useful preparation for teaching children the gymnastic skills of forward and backward rolls at a later stage.

After the warm-up, teachers might like to ask the children to try the following activities:

- stand in a stretched position with arms held high, followed by curling up into a tucked-up position, then stretching up again;
- stand with arms held high in the air, practice turning around on the spot, crouch down and practise turning on the spot;
- practise crouch jumps around a mat. Children should put their body weight on to two flat hands, and then transfer their weight to both feet;
- lie on their backs and practise rocking from side to side whilst in a tucked position;
- still in a tucked position, practise rocking from a sitting position backwards towards their shoulders;
- from a sitting position with heels close to bottoms, rock backwards and then try to use forward momentum to rock forwards to a standing position;
- lie in a stretched position and rock from one side of their bodies to the other, first whilst lying on their fronts and then whilst lying on their backs;
- roll in a pencil shape;
- roll in a tucked shape sideways.

Children who would normally be in wheelchairs should be allowed to practise these floor-based activities with adult manipulation.

All the children should be allowed to practise any of the activities outlined above in a free choice situation. Teachers can teach and guide those who need help in developing these skills. Children who become competent in these skills should be encouraged to make a movement pattern based on rocking, leading to the two rolls – forward and backward – being learned, and should be encouraged to make linking movements to complete their performance.

Cool-down ideas

- Stand still and stretch as tall as possible;
- make a wide star shape;
- hold own hands behind at the waist, behind knees and over right and left shoulders.

Travelling on hands and feet

'Travelling' covers the most basic actions which are essential to a gymnastic programme and which form the foundation of all physical activity. There is no doubt that the immature physical form of some reception class children can be developed by focusing on travelling on hands and feet.

Before the warm-up teachers should talk to the children again about the importance of warming up their bodies before beginning strenuous exercise. After the warm-up, teachers should introduce the children to the new theme and talk to them about why they think the activities the children will learn are important.

Once this has been done, teachers might then like to try out the following activities. These can be introduced in the order set down, a few activities each week. Some of the activities can be revisited, particularly if teachers have observed that some children are not yet competent.

Floorwork activities

- 'Show me different ways of travelling on your feet.' (Expect: walking, running, skipping, hopping, jogging, side-slipping, jumping, leaping. Encourage: long steps, short steps.)
- 'Show me the different parts of your feet which you can use to travel on.' (Expect: walking on toes, heels, sides of feet.)
- 'Show me all the different directions which you can travel.' (Expect: forwards, backwards, sideways, turning. Encourage: zig-zag, curved, diagonal pathways.)
- 'Can you travel on your feet at speed?' 'And slowly?'
- 'Can you travel near to the ground?'
- 'Show me all the ways you can travel on your hands and your feet.' (Expect: crawling and crouched jumps. Encourage: crawling with feet close together and then apart, crouched jumps with feet together and apart, the caterpillar walk: crouched position, keep feet still and crawl each hand forwards as far as possible. Then keep hands still and move the feet until they are near the hands; crab walk: face the ground, distribute body weight evenly on hands and feet and spread the limbs as wide as possible yet retaining stability, then walk sideways; turn over, face the ceiling and move backwards.)
- 'Can you travel on one hand and one foot?'

The children can be asked to make a movement pattern based on some of the activities.

Teachers could also ask children to try the following:

- 'Travel on your hands and feet along the floor and make a pattern which has three travelling movements in it, one which goes forwards, one which goes sideways and one which goes backwards. Try to link the movements.'
- 'Make a movement pattern which has three different ways of travelling on hands and feet in it. Can you repeat the pattern twice?'
- 'Make a movement pattern which shows two different turning actions whilst you are travelling on your hands and feet.'

Once the children have developed some expertise, hoops and ropes can be used to extend their capabilities. If the hoops are placed on the floor, the children can be asked to find ways of moving in and out of hoops on their hands and feet, or leaving their feet inside the hoop and moving their hands around the outside of the hoop, or travelling around the outside of the hoop on their hands and feet. Ropes can also be arranged in flexible patterns by the children and then used to practise some of the floorwork activities listed above.

When the children are showing competence in the skill of travelling on hands and feet they can transfer these skills on to the large apparatus. The apparatus selected should have large areas where the children can travel. Planks, gymnastic benches, suspended ladders, climbing frames and movement tables with large surface areas would be good choices. Planks, benches and ladders can be placed in front of apparatus or attached to it to form slopes, or suspended between two pieces of apparatus in a horizontal position. Teachers should look at each apparatus arrangement and consider what the children might do on it, so that they are sure that the skills which the children have learned can be transferred.

Teachers might like to suggest the following movement tasks:

- 'Explore your apparatus. Travel on, over, around and under it.'
- 'Move about your apparatus on your hands and feet. When you have finished, travel along the floor back to where you started.'
- 'Travel on your hands and feet as you did last week, but this time, travel backwards somewhere on your apparatus.'
- 'Travel on your hands and feet and, somewhere on the apparatus or when you are travelling on the floor, show me that you can travel quickly.'

As the children work, teachers should talk to each child and help him/her try different skills to increase the movement repertoire. All the children should eventually be able to show a good controlled starting position and a pattern of movement across the apparatus which links each separate skill together, shows good body shape and is completed with a controlled finish.

Children with disabling conditions of the legs could be allowed to work on the floor on mats and be given some arm-strengthening tasks to complete, or could be encouraged to use the floor surface to pull themselves along on their hands and arms. However, support staff should be reminded that lifting and carrying such children is a specialist technique and that specialist training should be acquired, and advice sought from a physiotherapist.

Cool-down ideas

- Lie on the floor and curl up, stretch out smoothly and slowly;
- stand still and stretch both arms high (North), both arms down towards feet (South), both arms to the right (East), both arms to the left (West). Teacher calls out North or South and so on;
- stand still and stretch arms out on a diagonal (one arm NE and the other SW).

Travelling on different body parts

This theme is connected to the gymnastic skills gained in two earlier themes, i.e., travelling on hands and feet and holding the body still on different body parts. The children can therefore build on these earlier experiences and develop some new combinations of skills which this theme will offer. After the warm-up, the teacher might ask the children to try the following activities:

- 'We have just spent a long time travelling on our hands and feet; can you find some other parts of your body to travel on?'
- 'Can you try all the ways which you can think of to travel on your feet? I can think of six different ways. Can you count them and let me know how many you find?'
- 'Can you travel around on your bottoms only? Try using your feet as well!'
- 'I saw somebody travelling on their lower legs. Can you try?'
- 'I wonder if you can find different ways of travelling on two parts of your body? We have already tried hands and feet, and bottoms and feet'
- 'Do you remember when we tried to hold our bodies still on different body parts? Perhaps that will help you to think of new ways?'

(Teacher's checklist: hands and feet, bottoms and feet, lower legs, knees and hands, hands and arms only with feet trailing (seal walk), backs and feet, one hand and one foot, elbows and knees, one elbow and one knee, sliding on stomach, rolling in a pencil roll, feet together and apart, rolling tucked up, travelling on feet in a star shape and a pencil shape.)

At this stage, the children should have an opportunity to use a combination of mats and gymnastic benches so that they can transfer and develop the skills which they have learned on the floor. For example, the use of gymnastic benches will give them a chance to pull and slide themselves on different parts of their bodies. They will also have an opportunity to link actions together into a simple sequence if they can take the travelling action from the bench to the mat and then continue it along the floor as they return to their starting place.

The large apparatus which is chosen for this theme should be erected so that there are both mats for rolling sideways on and surfaces to travel across, under, around and through.

Some suggestions for movement tasks could be:

- 'Explore your apparatus.'
- 'Travel on your apparatus and show me all the different parts of your body on which you can travel. You might not be able to show me all your ideas during your first turn.'
- 'Can you travel on, over, around or through your apparatus on your bottoms and feet only?'
- 'Somewhere on your travels, show me that you can travel on your knees and hands.'
- 'Choose the methods of travelling which you like best and make a linking movement sequence which takes you across your apparatus, along your mat, along the floor and back to where you started.'

Throughout all these activities, the children should be encouraged to plan their own sequence with the offer of help if they need it. They should practise the sequence which they have chosen and be ready to perform it for their peers. It must be remembered that children of this age cannot always remember what they did from week to week and so it is helpful for them if their teacher can highlight and evaluate effective planning and performance as it evolves.

Cool-down ideas

Teachers should remember to talk to the children about the reason for cool-down activities.

- Walk along floor on bottoms;
- sit with legs stretched and spine straight, and stretch fingers and toes;
- draw a large circle in the air, then draw a square, a rectangle and a triangle.

Stretching and curling the body

This theme is often used at all stages and with pupils of all ages in a gymnastic programme. It is a theme which helps children to develop an awareness of the simple movements which can change body shape and is very important since stretching, curling and twisting, for example, form the basis of all human movement. It also allows pupils to perform at their own level and as such it is a theme which can be introduced at any level and then can be revisited and developed throughout the whole of the National Curriculum in gymnastics. It might appear that some of the suggested gymnastic activities have been explored in previous thematic programmes but it is important to note that here the context is different and by choosing this context it is possible to link all the themes so far discussed so that the children can finally bring together all the work of their Year 1 gymnastic activities Programme of Study.

Suggested activities

After the warm-up the teacher can take the children through the following activities by suggesting that they:

- stretch high in the air followed by curling up in a tucked position . . . Use various speeds, sometimes explode into a high stretched shape, sometimes grow slowly into a stretched shape;
- stretch into an irregular shape, holding it, then curl into a tucked shape;
- stretch wide and curl into a tucked shape;
- lie on the floor and stretch and curl (give the children an opportunity to choose their own shapes);
- run around the area with arms stretched high in the air, then stretched out wide;
- walk in a tucked shape, and jump along whilst in a tucked shape;
- walk with legs wide, then sit with legs stretched out wide;
- sit with legs tucked in, then explode with legs and arms out wide!
- sit and spin around with legs curled in and then legs stretched out;
- travel on hands and feet, keeping the body stretched;
- choose a body part to be still on and then stretch all the other parts;
- choose a body part to be still on, then curl up all the other parts;
- hop on one foot whilst stretching spines and feet and legs which are in the air;
- skip along with a stretched spine and stretched lower legs.

The children should be encouraged to perform all the above activities with good body shape and with good quality movements.

Sutcliffe (1996) has stated that time in PE is precious. Children, she suggests, plan and evaluate as they practise and perform many everyday physical tasks quite instinctively, but in the PE lesson it is the focus given during the practise of a movement which is so valuable. In this theme it is suggested that the focus should initially be on ensuring that the children show the best body shape of which they are capable as they complete their movements. As they do this, the teacher needs to make careful observations so that each child can be encouraged to stretch a little more, or curl up more tightly in order to create a good body shape. The children will soon make progress if teachers are willing to give them a clear understanding of what it is they are looking for in their performances. Teachers should also use a demonstration technique to show the children what the the focus of the performance should be. They can do this by choosing a child who is already performing movements at the required standard, and who can show specific examples of the type of stretched positions and shapes which constitute good performance. Teachers can also guide all the children's developing ability to express themselves clearly by encouraging them to evaluate their peers' performances verbally.

Once the children are performing good quality movements on the floor they can then be gathered into groups of four or five to begin to work on large apparatus. Once again the layout should be planned with care so that pieces of equipment are chosen which will give all the children an opportunity to work within the theme.

Suggested movement tasks might be:

- 'Explore your apparatus' (if the apparatus is set out satisfactorily, and if the children have reached a competent standard of floorwork, the children should begin to use stretching and curling movements as they use the apparatus).
- 'Which of the stretching and curling movements can you show me on the apparatus?'
- 'Choose the stretching and curling movements which you like best and practise them across the apparatus and on the floor, returning to your apparatus.'
- 'Choose the movements which you like best and link them together to make a movement pattern.'

Cool-down ideas

Teachers can talk to the children about the importance of having good body posture in all that they do in every-day activities.

- Sit with legs crossed, spine straight and head held erect;
- sit with good posture with legs and feet stretched;
- stand up with good posture, walk with good posture.

There is no statutory requirement for teachers to assess the children's work at the end of Year 1, but there is, however, a requirement to report to parents. Teachers will have assembled a mass of knowledge about the children in their class and if they have been using the skill development checklist (page 62) they will know whether their children have made progress. Since continuity is vital, it goes without saying that the teacher must pass on this knowledge to the Year 2 teacher. For some children, too, information must be given to the parents so that special help can be provided.

GYMNASTIC ACTIVITIES FOR YEAR 2

Before beginning to plan the scheme of work and the lesson content which will complete the Programme of Study for the children in Key Stage 1, it is very important that the incoming teacher talks to those who have already taught the children in Year 1. This is obviously necessary for continuity purposes but it is especially important for those children who have special needs so that their condition is known and, if necessary, special intervention procedures can be put in place for them. It would also be worthwhile at this point to consider the End of Key Stage Description for Key Stage 1 before any practical decisions are made in connection with teaching. The End of Key Stage Description tells us, for example, that:

Pupils plan and perform simple skills safely, and show control in linking actions together. They improve their performance through practising their skills, working alone and with a partner. They talk about what they and others have done, and are able to make simple judgements. They recognise and describe the changes that happen to their bodies during exercise.

(Department for Education and Employment 1995: 11)

The possibility of links with other subject areas is worthwhile considering, too, before work is started in Physical Education.Work taking place in science, for instance, might mean that at this stage children have more time to deepen their understanding of the 'changes that occur in their bodies as they exercise, to recognise the short-term effects of exercise on the body' and the importance of 'physical activity' in developing 'healthy lifestyles' (ibid.: 3, 2).

Before work in the gymnastic activities area of activity begins with Year 2 children, all the necessary pre-planning should be done in the same way as for Year 1. As far as the detail of approaches to 'theme' teaching is concerned the basic format of lessons should remain the same, i.e., warm-up, practical activities and cool-down. However, aspects of the Programme of Study which have not yet been covered should be included in the scheme of work, and 'common aspects' which can be included in all three areas of activity, i.e., games, dance and gymnastic activities, should also be considered for inclusion.

The gymnastic skills which children need to learn in Year 2 are the following:

- travelling using hands and feet;
- rolling and sliding;
- swinging, climbing, spinning, turning;
- balancing;
- jumping and landing.

Each theme should allow the children to be taught the 'different ways of performing the basic actions' (*ibid.*) outlined in the list above.

Travelling on hands and feet

This theme was covered in Year 1 and so can be revisited at the beginning of Year 2, using exactly the kind of approach as previously (see pages 80–3). The children will be familiar with the activities which constitute the theme of work and should therefore feel more confident as they begin to work with a new teacher. As work proceeds, teachers will have an opportunity to assess the children and also ensure that they are aware of any children who have special needs and that proper provision has been made for them to take a full and active part in the lessons.

Rolling and sliding

The rolling activities which were practised in Year 1 will have given the children a basic understanding of one of the fundamental skills which form the sport of gymnastics (see page 79). It is interesting to observe that tumbling has become an important event in school gymnastics competitions and many children who attend gymnastics clubs will have become proficient in performing rolling skills. Rolling or somersaulting around apparatus is an important skill which can be developed through this theme. For some children, though, the actions of rolling, sliding and somersaulting will be new activities and so due care must be taken for their physical safety. The warm-up must be carefully structured to ensure that the body is properly prepared for the work to be accomplished. The basic principles outlined earlier (see pages 61, 71–2) still apply, but there should be an added focus as work progresses on developing flexibility in the spine.

During Year 1, the children will have spent a number of weeks moving on their hands and feet over different surfaces and so should have increased their arm strength, an important ingredient in the successful completion of the forward roll and backward roll. The following sequence, then, following the warm-up, would be a useful development of the work at this stage.

Floorwork activities

- Rocking and rolling activities from the Year 1 programme;
- arm-strengthening activities:

    (i) caterpillar: from a crouched position, keep feet still and walk hands across the floor until the legs and spine are fully stretched; then, keeping the hands still, walk the feet forwards until a crouched position is achieved; repeat;

    (ii) kicking donkey; both hands flat on the floor, arms straight, kick legs in the air;

    (iii) seal walk: put hands on floor and keep arms straight; stretch body out, and keeping legs straight and feet stretched, use hands and arms to move around the area;

    (iv) clockwork: prone position, feet still, use hands to move around the floor through 360 degrees – the face of a clock;

    (v) clap hands: prone position, weight evenly distributed on two feet and two hands, clap hands!

- crouch jumps around a mat;
- pushing and pulling themselves around the mat when in a prone position;
- linking rolling sideways with sliding movements.

Group the children together and give each group two mats. Arrange the mats so that there is a space between them of about 2 metres and ask the children to roll sideways across the first mat, slide along the floor and roll sideways across the second mat. Objectives here would be to encourage the children to think of good starting positions, to keep a good body shape whilst rolling and to try and link the movements together. Each of these three elements of good quality performance should be focused on one at a time.

The backward roll

There is no statutory requirement in the National Curriculum that children should be able to complete any specific roll and some teachers may not feel confident that they can keep their children safe when teaching anything other than sideways tucked and pencil rolls. However, teachers should seriously consider teaching the backward roll which can undoubtedly be taught safely to children, who in their turn will then be able to practise at home.

A useful way of building up the skills needed would be for the children, first of all, to practise rocking from their bottoms to their shoulders. As they do this, teachers should make sure that the children tuck their legs in and place their hands on the floor at either side of their heads with their elbows bent. Emphasis should be placed on the rocking action towards the shoulders and the hand position which can be called 'rabbit ears', i.e., the children should put their hands at the sides of their ears, left thumb touching the left ear and the right thumb touching the right ear with the palms of the hands facing forwards. Second, when rocking backwards, the children should keep their spines rounded and their elbows bent. The palms of their hands should face the ceiling, ready to push on to the floor at the sides of their heads at the end of the rocking action. When they eventually have the confidence to do the backward roll they should start in a crouched position on their feet, roll backwards through sitting on to their shoulders, and then push down hard on their hands to keep the backwards momentum going and to take their bodies over their heads. As their hands touch the floor they should thrust and extend their arms to get their hips high and allow a clearance for their head. They should lift their heads quickly and return to their feet.

The forward roll

To accomplish the forward roll correctly and safely, the children will need to have some knowledge of how to control their body weight, and an awareness of body tension and strong arms. It is also very important to remember that children of this age should never practise this activity without individual adult supervision. For teachers with many children to supervise, one way of overcoming this problem would be to provide a thick mat as one of the apparatus group activities in the large apparatus experience within the theme. If the mat is placed strategically, teachers can then attend to the supervision of the practice of forward rolling while, at the same time, having a full view of all the other children.

Initially, children should be asked which type of roll they would like to try, so that they have a choice about whether they would like to learn the skill at this time. Naturally, teachers will know which children are capable of being persuaded otherwise!

The method for teaching the forward roll is, first, to tell the children to stand off the mat, and spread their legs wide. They should lean forwards with their arms extended and their hands ready to take some of their body weight. Then they should tuck their heads between their legs (they can be asked to, 'look through your legs') and fall forwards, pushing with their hands so that their body weight rests on their shoulders.The completion of the roll follows almost automatically. In the early stages of learning this skill, teachers can help the children by putting one of their arms along the child's spine and helping them to curl it. The children could also start the roll by taking up a crouched position on their feet; from this position they should lean forward with their arms extended until their hands touch the floor. At the same time, they should thrust their feet off the floor to start a forwards momentum, tuck their heads in, round their spines, bend their knees, tuck their feet in near their hips and reach forwards with their hands. The hands should be placed flat on the floor and there should be a strong push downwards as the body starts to rotate and the hips and then the legs come over the head. To gain the standing position after rolling the children must make sure that their heels are close to their bottoms and that their arms are reaching upwards and forwards.

Apparatus for rolling activities

This apparatus (bench, plank, mat) should be set out so that each group has a bench or a plank, to push, pull or slide on and a mat on which to roll sideways. The suggested movement tasks used in conjunction with the apparatus are as follows:

- ask the children to explore the apparatus and show you where they can push, pull and slide their bodies, and where they can complete a sideways roll;
- let the children visit each apparatus grouping and try the task above;
- ask the children to choose where they would like to work and ask them to plan a movement pattern which has linked movements which shows their ability to roll and slide. The children should be encouraged to start at different places on the apparatus, to use the floor and to keep working all the time;
- ask the children if they would like to rearrange their apparatus and encourage them to say why.

Once the children have created a movement pattern, teachers should talk to the children about improving their performance by adding quality to their work. The idea here would be to focus on one aspect until the children have acquired the required standard, for example:

- 'Where are you going to start? What body position are you going to have?'
- 'Do all your movements link together?'
- 'How are you going to finish? Where are you going to finish your pattern?'
- 'Is the shape of your body clear all the time?'

Each lesson should end with a cool-down after the children have put the apparatus away.

Cool-down ideas

- Lie down on the floor and stretch the body, then relax it;
- stand up and walk with good body posture;

- stretch arms high above the head;
- bend the right leg, hold the right toes with the left hand in front of the body, then behind the body.

Swinging, climbing, spinning and turning

This theme is concerned with four of the basic actions listed in the National Curriculum Programme of Study. All the basic actions of swinging, climbing, spinning and turning are fundamental movements which children can enjoy in gymnastic activities lessons. Learning and practising the particular actions of swinging and climbing might be difficult depending on the type of large apparatus which schools can provide. If this becomes a problem, one way of solving it would be to take the class to the local playground for one or two sessions so that the children can experience the kinaesthetic pleasure associated with these two skills. Lessons incorporating these actions might proceed as follows: after the warm-up, the children can be asked to try the following activities:

- 'Walk around the space. On a signal, turn and walk in another direction.'
- 'run, and on a signal, turn and run in another direction' (Use the same command for skipping, then hopping, then jumping).
- 'Sit down and spin around and around.'
- 'Stand up and spin around and around.'
- 'Lie on the floor and turn over and over.'
- 'Distribute your body weight evenly on your hands and your feet. Can you turn over?' (Face the floor, then face the ceiling.)
- 'Swing your arms at the sides of your body.'
- 'Swing your arms across your body.'
- 'Stand on both feet, jump and turn to face the opposite way (180 degrees).'
- 'Use sideways slipping steps, to move to the right, and without stopping, turn and sidestep the other way.'
- 'Jump into a hoop, turn and jump out again.'
- 'Spin round on your bottom inside the hoop.'
- 'Leap over your hoop, turn and leap back to your starting position.'
- 'Both feet together, swing your arms at the sides of your body, bend your knees and jump over your hoop, turn and repeat the action.'
- 'Hold a partner's hands, lean backwards to support each other's body weight and spin around and around.'
- 'Jump over your partner, turn and return to start (partner to curl up on the floor).'
- 'Crawl over your partner, do not touch!'
- 'Run as fast as you can to your partner, turn and walk back to starting place.'

- 'Crawl under the bridge shapes made by your partner.'
- 'Move by using crouched jumps ("bunny jumps"). Can you move quickly? Can you lift your hips higher in the air?'
- 'Show me a caterpillar crawl; stretch as far as you can and hold the position before walking your hands towards your feet.'
- 'Show me three movements – a spinning movement, a turning movement and a swinging movement.'
- 'Can you link a series of these actions to make a movement pattern? Can you repeat it?'

Next, set up the the the apparatus so that the children can practise the four basic actions of climbing, turning, swinging and spinning.

Movement tasks

- 'Choose where you would like to be on the apparatus, make sure that you have enough space and that you can start working straight away. Find out where you can complete the actions of climbing, or swinging, or turning or spinning.' (The children should be asked if they would like to rearrange the apparatus so that they can complete their actions more successfully.)
- 'Find places where you can turn around on your apparatus.'
- 'Find places where you can turn over on your apparatus.'
- 'Can you spin anywhere on your apparatus?'
- 'If you are on a climbing frame, have you tried turning around on it or climbing across it? Can you swing anywhere?'
- 'Choose where you want to work and plan a movement pattern which has three of the basic actions which we have been practising in it. You can use the floor as well as the apparatus.'

Cool-down ideas

- Stretch into any shape, hold it and count to five;
- walk around the space with good posture;
- sit with your legs stretched out and touch your toes.

The work suggested for this theme should give teachers plenty of time to observe the children and to assess whether they can fulfil the requirements listed in the End of Key Stage Descriptions.

Balancing

The children will have worked on 'holding the body still on different body parts' in Year 1 and this work can be revisited (see pages 73–6) before proceeding to new work on balancing. Revisiting the previous theme will give teachers an opportunity to assess the children's abilities and to judge when they think new work can be introduced.

The theme of balance runs through all the four key stages in the National Curriculum gymnastic programme and so will be offered to children as part of a whole and progressive structure. In Year 2, children will be introduced to the concept of balancing their bodies on large and small bases. It may be the case that the children will have some knowledge of this concept from the weighing activities with which they will have been involved in the classroom, or from see-saw activities, balance walking activities, etc., which they will have experienced in pre-school.

A short warm-up can be followed by moving on to the floorwork activities.

Floorwork suggestions

- 'Stand on one leg without wobbling.' (Talk with the children about moving their body weight over on to the central base of one foot.)
- 'Balance on your bottom, lift your feet and arms off the floor!'
- 'Balance on one lower leg.'
- 'Balance on two hands and one foot, then two feet and one hand.'
- 'Balance on one foot and one hand.'
- 'Balance on one knee and one elbow.'
- 'Which other small parts of your body can you balance on?'
- 'Can you balance with a straight leg on one foot and make a "T" shape by leaning forward and stretching out both arms and one leg?'
- 'What other body shapes can you make when you are balancing?' (On one foot, one knee, bottom, lower back.)
- 'Balance on your shoulders.' (From a lying position lift legs and bottom in the air, pointing toes to the ceiling, bend each elbow and tuck into the sides of the body, support hips on hands.)
- 'Can you put your legs in different places when you are balancing on your shoulders?'
- 'Can you balance on your stomach?' (Lift upper torso and legs off the floor.)
- 'Can you make different body shapes when you are balancing on your stomach?'

Having completed the floorwork, the Year 2 children could then be taught a headstand – a good 'balancing' skill. Mats should be used for this practice and initially children should be shown how to make a triangular base with the hairline pressed into the mat and both hands, palms down with the fingers facing forwards. (The head and each hand should be equal distances apart and form the three points of an equilateral triangle.)

At this point the body will be in a crouched position. The children should hold their position and walk their feet forwards, keeping their spines straight, and pushing down on to the ground with equal pressure on the head and the hands. When the body weight is almost entirely transferred on to the hands and head, and the hips are almost directly over the head, the children should bend their legs and gently let their feet leave the ground so that they are in an inverted tuck position, and then slowly straighten their legs. Once they have completed the headstand the children should bend their knees, ground their feet and return to the crouched position. Incidentally, it is easier for children, always assuming that they have the confidence, to try this skill if there is a suitable soft play cube to practise against (or the couch at home). The mats can also be used to help those children who are not confident to balance on the floor to make progress by providing a soft base on which to work. At the same time, 'gifted' children can have their work extended by asking them to develop their work on smaller balancing bases.

At this stage of development, most children should be able to show their ability to fulfil the specific requirements of the gymnastic activities Programme of Study which calls for them to be able to plan and perform a series of linked movements. Such a task would be built around the basic action of balancing. A possible way of developing this would be to ask the children to make a movement pattern which shows their ability to balance on three different parts of their bodies and to find interesting ways of moving from one balance to another. After having accomplished this, it would be important to let the children share the resultant performances with their peers and give them the opportunity to evaluate their own and other children's performances.

Large apparatus tasks for balancing

- 'Explore your apparatus.'
- 'Choose a place on the apparatus where you can balance on one part of your body. Use interesting movements to get on and get off the apparatus and make sure you balance for at least a count of ten.'
- 'Choose three places on the apparatus where you can balance on one part of your body – it can be the same part or three different parts. Link the balances with interesting movements. Can you do it again?'

Teachers should encourage the children to plan, practise and refine their chosen movement pattern and be ready to perform it. Teachers will have allowed the children to make their own choices about the type of movements which they complete, but they should all be in no doubt that whatever they have chosen to do it must be performed with good quality. There should be a starting position and a finishing position which demonstrate the children's abilities to hold their bodies in stillness with good posture. All the movements which link the balances should be completed with the required amount of speed and tension and should show a good range of muscle use. The balance positions chosen should be held in stillness, showing extension of the limbs, particularly the fingers and toes.

Cool-down ideas

- Crouch down and put your weight equally on your hands and your feet, press down onto the floor;
- walk around without making a sound;
- sit down and stand up as smoothly and as slowly as possible.

Jumping and landing

Before this theme, teachers should spend the first few lessons in ensuring that the children are 'resilient', i.e., that they are capable of controlling their body weight safely when they land from various activities which have taken them into the air. To this end, children should be taught about the joints in their hips, knees, ankles and feet which allow them to land from heights if used properly and should be given many, many activities which allow them the opportunity to reinforce this concept.

After a suitable warm-up, the children's understanding can be developed by working on floorwork activities such as:

- hopping on one foot, then the other;
- leaping over magic spots (emphasis on bending hips, knees, ankles and toes);
- hopping on magic spots, jumping up and down with two feet together on the magic spot;
- jumping around the magic spot with two feet together, forwards and backwards;
- jumping over EDRA cubes and cylinders;
- jumping over consecutive spots, then cubes or cylinders;
- running and leaping, running and leaping and landing on two feet;
- jumping from two feet to two feet whilst moving forwards, then backwards;
- one-footed take-off to leap over a curled-up partner, then free running and leaping over other people's partners;
- jumping into a hoop and out again moving forwards, then with a turn to land;
- jumping into a hoop held 5cms off the ground and stepping out again;
- run, jump in the air and land, try different take-offs, different shapes in the air, different landings;
- run and jump in the air and land on a mat, then with a half-turn in the air to land facing take-off position.

All these activities should be followed by many practices of landing from low heights and jumping over small obstacles, mainly to practise landing safely. Teachers should keep emphasising the need to bend all the joints and it might be useful to use appropriate comparisons such as 'like Zebedee', or 'like a bouncy ball', or 'like Gromit's bunjee jumping' or even 'like bouncing on your bed' to make the point!

Incidentally, benches and EDRA logs are useful pieces of equipment to use so that children can progress gradually through the stages of learning to control their body weight as it descends from a height. If they are used, a mat should be placed at the end of the bench/log when children are asked to:

- walk along the bench and step off; then jump off on to their mat;
- step over the bench, and then leap over and, for some, jump over;
- jump along the bench with two feet together (speed differentiated according to ability);
- run along and jump off the end (some will choose to walk) to land on the mat;
- stand with legs astride the bench and jump along forwards.

The large apparatus chosen for developing this skill should allow each child to jump and land from a height of their choosing. Table tops and gymnastic stools and boxes, for example, should be of different heights. There should always be plenty of space for those children who want to mount the apparatus after a run to do this, and there should also be space for the children to land safely from all equipment. Mats should be placed wherever the children will be expected to land from a height. If some children prefer to continue their climbing practices rather than practise jumping and landing, then they should be encouraged to jump down from the lowest rung from a one-handed–two-footed position.

In all the lessons the emphasis should be on controlling body weight both when in the air and on landing. Some children may work on low-level equipment such as a bench and a mat, whilst others may work on a high gymnastic table, but wherever they choose to work the outcome should always be the same, i.e., good body position at take-off, whilst moving or in the air, and on landing. In this theme, the ultimate focus must always be the safe control of the body weight.

Cool-down ideas

- Follow my leader. Do what the teacher does (in silence);
- 'Head and shoulders, knees and toes' (completed in silence).

Teachers must report to parents at the end of the key stage and should also communicate with the teacher who will teach the children during Year 3.

The links between the teachers are of paramount importance for the children if progression is to be achieved. The End of Key Stage Descriptions form the skeleton of the structure for reporting purposes.

Chapter 5

Games in Key Stage 1

The detailed blueprint *Sport: Raising the Game* (Department of National Heritage 1995) sets out an agenda for the future of sport in Great Britain. In the introduction to this document John Major articulates his desire 'to put sport back at the heart of weekly life in *every* school' (p. 2). He maintains that 'Sport is a binding force between generations and across borders. But, by a miraculous paradox, it is at the same time one of the defining characteristics of nationhood and local pride. We should cherish it for both those reasons.' He goes on to say: 'In this initiative I put the highest priority on plans to help all our schools improve their sport. Sport is open to all ages – but it is most open to those who learn to love it when they are young' (p. 3).

Prior to 1995, the Physical Education Working Group made the following statement:

> Competitive games, both individual and team, are an essential part of any programme of physical education. They are part of our national heritage and offer a range of educational opportunities. To explore to the full those opportunities it is necessary to offer pupils a balance of games experiences.
>
> (Department of Education and Science 1991: 75)

The National Curriculum Programme of Study document which is concerned with the area of activity called 'games' quite clearly maintains that pupils in Key Stage 1 should be taught:

    a simple competitive games, including how to play them as individuals and when ready, in pairs and in small groups;

    b to develop and practise a variety of ways of sending (including throwing, striking, rolling and bouncing), receiving and travelling with a ball and other similar games equipment;

    c elements of games play that include running, chasing, dodging, avoiding and awareness of space and other players.

                                  (Department for Education and Employment 1995: 3)

It would appear then that the government, Physical Education specialists and the Department for Education are all agreed that an area of activity, which John Major calls 'sport' and which educationists call 'games', is a very important element in the National Curriculum. However, it is very important to know exactly what the terminology being used is specifically about. It would appear, for example, that according to John Major 'sport in school' means taking part in team games, whereas it is more than likely that a physical educationist, if required to teach 'sport' in schools, would have a broader agenda which would include individual sports such as athletics, tennis and swimming. Traditionally, games would have been a subject taught in schools, whilst sport would be a pastime to be indulged in leisure time. Whatever one's interpretation it is obvious that there is an overlap in meaning, so it is important to say that for the purposes of what follows, 'games' is to be used in its collective sense of children playing together in a team situation and both using and building upon particular physical skills which they have learned along the way.

It is interesting to observe that throughout this century 'games' in an education context have been used as a vehicle for many different social purposes. One of the earliest was to try and develop young people's moral principles through the use of games playing. Later, games were used to engender team spirit and co-operation, whilst during the last decade, and even now, games playing is considered to be one of the activities which promotes an active and healthy lifestyle. A careful analysis of the current Programme of Study for Physical Education, shows that it contains many of these desired outcomes. For instance, the General Requirements for Physical Education Key Stages 1–4 state that:

> To develop positive attitudes pupils should be taught:
>
> a to observe the conventions of fair play and honest competition and good sporting behaviour as team members, individual participants and spectators;
> b how to cope with success and failure;
> c to try hard to consolidate their performances;
> d to be mindful of others and the environment.

(Department for Education and Employment 1995: 2)

Games has also been a value-added activity in many schools where young people have been offered the playing of games as an extra-curricular activity. Many teachers have been inspirational in giving children a 'love' of games by instilling them with their own enthusiasms. The National Curriculum does not preclude this type of input from teachers and it is clear that John Major himself values it when he talks about the need to inspire children to learn the love of games when they are young. In following the statutory Programme of Study then, teachers can feel confident that it will give their children the fundamental basis for developing their games skill learning. Unfortunately, however, it will not guarantee that children will develop a 'love' of games which will of course depend on the children, their home culture and the enthusiasm of the teacher!

Before beginnning to teach games at Key Stage 1 teachers will need to think quite carefully about how they plan to approach the task. The content of the scheme of work for Key Stage 1 should be built around a whole school policy and as with the other areas of activity discussed previously, should build on the work which the children will have covered in their pre-schools. There is plenty of practical help available at this level. There are many schemes of work for games which have been compiled by LEAs which schools can adopt as part of their whole school policy for games, and there are also two national schemes which can be used as additional resources. One such has been initiated by the Sports Council, working in partnership with the Youth Sports Trust, which has launched (1996) a national Junior Sports Programme which includes a new games resource called Top Play.

Top Play is designed for 4–9 year olds and focuses on core games skills. The programme has been launched with a simple philosophy, 'selling sport to children'. The scheme is intended to integrate with other games schemes and individual school plans, and will only be effective if integrated into the whole school planning for PE.

(Sports Council 1996: 8–9).

The other scheme is produced by the Physical Education Association of the United Kingdom. (PEAUK) and is called PEGS (Physical Education Games Scheme). Both these national resources offer a variety of progressive activities, which can be set up easily, and which are related to, and support the requirements of the National Curriculum.

Help, admittedly of a less practical nature, but nevertheless welcome, comes from several authors who have written informed texts which include more detailed information about games playing and games making in Key Stage 1. Much of the information is concerned with the rationale behind teaching children to play games. Amongst such texts is the work of Cooper (1995) who is explicit in discussing the principles of developing games skills in children of this age, and who gives a concise analysis of how Key Stage 1 children learn them. He discusses the principles of progression and the importance of a planning structure. Bunker (Bunker, Hardy, Smith and Almond 1994: 90) gives a brief rationale for the inclusion of 'games making' as an important feature of a games education. He believes that children of this age should be given opportunities to make up games because this allows them to work at their own level of physical skill, and to explore ways in which a variety of equipment might be used. He offers clear suggestions for those teachers who prefer to use this method to achieve the End of Key Stage learning outcomes suggested in the National Curriculum.

Heath *et al.*, (1994) argue that the key feature of playing games is the development of motor skills, hand–eye co-ordination and strategies linked to playing games. They offer teachers a compendium of lesson plans which are grouped into units of work which can be used across the Key Stage 1 games curriculum, whilst Read and Edwards (1992: 9) offer the concept of a games curriculum 'spiral', showing teachers how skills are first established and then adapted or refined to respond to more complex games and tighter rules, faster play and the need for individuals to adopt specialist roles. Their games teaching resource is intended for those teaching children aged 5–11. Thirty of the pages in their ring-file of information is focused on 'familiarisation' for Key Stage 1 and the other 201 pages are aimed at pupils in Key Stage 2, thus providing teachers with an opportunity to cross key stage boundaries if such exist. Thus, there is considerable choice for teachers, not only in choosing the content for a scheme of work which will fulfil the requirements of the games area of activity but also in knowing what children at this stage are capable of in the PE Programme of Study.

Unfortunately, however, it is a much more difficult task for teachers of young children to teach a well-structured games programme than to choose the content of the curriculum. Ironically, the children themselves are central to the planning of the curriculum and they can pose some difficult problems at this age for teachers in the particular ways they respond to games teaching. The reasons for this are complex. First, it must be remembered that children of this age are still coming to terms with their developing selves as personal and social individuals. As Dowling reminds us: 'Children are also affected by the context in which learning takes place, the people involved in it, and the values and beliefs which are embedded in it' (Department of Education and Science 1990: paras 67–8). Second, and as has been stated earlier in the book, children come into statutory schooling from many different pre-school settings, which may already have had a particular effect on them intellectually, socially and emotionally. Third, a consideration which has also been articulated earlier, are the special needs which children bring to the learning environment. All these concerns must be taken into account when beginning to structure a games scheme of work.

In practical terms, then, the teacher may be faced with structuring a games programme for children who will probably not have had a common past experience. As Dowling (1995) comments, although the learning which children will have acquired before statutory schooling will be immense, the range of their experiences will be very different. She also points out that sound acquisition of new learning is always dependent on what is known already, and that sound teaching is dependent on the teacher having made an assessment of what has previously been learned. Consulting pre-school records and communicating with pre-school teachers would therefore seem to be a priority before any scheme of work for games can be created for Key Stage 1.

The complex requirements which each child brings to the games lesson are many, but it is probably the child's social abilities which can be the most difficult to harness. Four and 5-year-olds can be notoriously ego-centric, and it is this aspect which can lead to management problems for teachers when they begin to teach the children. OFSTED stresses that the quality of children's relationships are central for forming children's attitudes to co-operation, social behaviour and self-discipline. Children of this age can develop these qualities if they are nurtured in a games environment in which effort is praised, encouragement is given and where adults show good role models. In view of this, the logical step in considering the method or methods to be used would be to ensure that the children are happy in their learning. There seems no point in promoting a games programme which children do not enjoy, since the grandiose claims about the social value which can be acquired from learning through games will not be fulfilled if the children do not have fun! As Armstrong and McManus (1996: 31) have advised: 'If we want children to take on activity as part of their lifestyle, then they have to be shown that exercise is fun.'

Fun in games is therefore suggested as the basis for the development of both games skills, social skills and personal development. The competitive aspects of games playing can be introduced through this fun and games approach. Pepitone (1993: 3–4) has warned us that: 'Competition becomes more powerful as the stakes become higher; the fun and games of early childhood often turn to deadly contests. By definition, where rewards are limited, some must be losers.' If teachers accept this, then teaching methods can be chosen which bring in the competitive element gradually, so that the children can be protected from being losers, or if they are to be losers, they all lose together! For example, the whole class may compete against the teacher as in the example of the bean bag game, or in the game 'What time is it Mr. Wolf?' Competition can also be introduced which is set up so that the children compete against themselves, e.g., kicking a ball to hit a target, or, after succeeding, trying to knock the target down three times in succession.

As far as methodology is concerned, it was suggested in the last chapter that a variety of teaching methods could be used at different times, during the span of a scheme of work. Similarly in games teaching: sometimes the whole class will play games with the teacher; whilst at other times the children would play alongside each other so that they could develop their games skills at their own rate of learning; and finally, the children could play relay games to develop the feeling of 'team'. All these methods can be used to deliver the curriculum for the Key Stage 1 games programme, with the inclusion of the development of playing games with a partner or in a group.

Teachers will know about how children grow and develop and will therefore know which games skills should be taught first. The material in this chapter is not set down as two specific programmes for each year, but is structured around a 'hierarchy of skills' approach to the teaching of games, based on the developmental approach to children's learning. Each skill listed below follows a developmental pattern and it is suggested that they are taught in the order in which they are listed. However, the value of repetition and the revisiting of skills should always be remembered, so children who have followed the games programme suggested in the last chapter should now proceed to learn the following.

Travelling skills

- Running and stopping on a signal;
- running and jumping;
- hopping and skipping;
- running, stopping and turning;
- dodging.

Sending skills

- Rolling a ball (size 4) to hit a target;
- throwing a ball (size 4) underarm, across the space;
- throwing various sized and shaped balls in all directions through the air for accuracy;
- throwing a size 4 ball for distance;
- kicking a ball (size 4);
- kicking a ball (size 4) for accuracy at a target;
- throwing a ball (size 4) into, or through, hoops, rings or circles.

Travelling skills with equipment

- Dribbling a ball (size 4) with the feet;
- bouncing a ball (size 4) whilst travelling forwards;
- running around obstacles whilst carrying different shaped balls.

Receiving skills

- Receive a rolling ball (size 4) or quoit;
- receive a large ball which has bounced a few times;

- receive a large ball which has bounced once;
- bounce and catch a large ball (size 4);
- throw a ball in the air underarm, let it bounce, and catch (size 4);
- stop a large ball with feet or hands;
- catch a large ball coming from the air, thrown by self.

Incidentally, games lessons should take place outdoors wherever possible, so that the children are not restricted in the practice of their games skills. There is also a 'feel-good factor' after playing in the fresh air which the children – and the teacher – will enjoy. It is also valuable for children to play on the surfaces and in the environment which they will use during school playtimes, so that they can be more confident when they are active during these periods. Any playground markings or any fixed equipment which are available for the children's free choice of play at playtimes can also be brought into use during PE lessons outdoors for the same reasons.

In view of this, several safety factors need consideration when children play games in the playground. For instance, the surface of the play area should be even, and be free from loose grit. Concrete, incidentally, is considered to be too hard for playing games. Steep slopes and sudden changes in ground level should also be avoided and if grass is used it should be dry. There should be enough space for the children to be active all the time. There should be no protrusions which might cause an accident. At a personal level, children should wear both safe footwear and suitable clothing, whilst long hair should be tied back. Jewellery should be removed and those children who wear glasses should be persuaded to have unbreakable lenses. During games lessons, as in all PE lessons, teachers should stand in a position where they can see all the children all of the time. If a playground is used then it should be marked out specifically to assist teachers to manage the children in games lessons. One idea suggested by Cooper (1995: 12) is that there should be four colour-coded areas to aid organisation. Another idea would be to have colour-coded assembly corners.

Teachers are often prevented from teaching games because of the difficult access which prevails in some situations. Organising thirty children to move from a classroom through corridors and out to the play space can be a formidable task. If the need to collect various pieces of equipment is added to this then it is easy to understand why teachers so seldom go outside for a games lesson with young children. One way to obviate difficulties here would be to store the equipment on a trolley, and to store balls in special bag containers (available from specialist equipment suppliers; see resources section). At one time even this suggestion caused problems since so many schools have entry steps, but now that children with special needs are being educated in mainstream schools, ramps have been provided for children using wheelchairs – a useful facility for wheeling games trolleys outside too!

However, the first time that teachers take children outside – and also for one or two subsequent lessons – they might find it easier not to take out any equipment at all so that they can concentrate on managing the children and teaching them any rules concerned with moving through the school, for example, walking without talking, monitors to hold doors and so on. Once they are outside, they can then focus on teaching the children aspects of games playing which do not need equipment. In all cases, all teachers should ensure that the children have a suitable warm-up, where they not only prepare their bodies for skill learning activities, but where they learn to listen to signals and listen to information.

Warm-up game suggestions

1 'Run anywhere you like, but when you hear my whistle, freeze! I shall be looking to see who is still wobbling!'
2 'Run around and when I call three names, people with those names, stop running and jump on the spot, whilst everyone else keeps running. When new names are called the former jumpers become runners, and so on.'
3 The 'Bean game' (see page 73).
4 The 'Body part game' (see page 73).
5 'Colour corners.' Four different coloured bean bags are placed, one in each corner, for colour identification. The children are asked to run anywhere, and on a signal, to choose one corner to stand in. Teachers turn their backs and choose a colour; all the children in that corner are caught out! They enter the new game straight away. Children in Year 2 have been observed to be capable of taking the teacher's role during this game
6 'Tig.' Child A stands still whilst Child B runs away. On a signal from the teacher Child A chases Child B and tries to 'tig' Child B.
7 'Tig 2.' Child B stands behind Child A, and follows Child A wherever Child A goes. On a signal Child B runs away and Child A chases and tries to tig Child B.
8 'Statues.' One half of the class stands still whilst their partners run in the spaces between them. On a signal from the teacher the children who are running, stop, look for their partners, and run to stand next to them as quickly as possible.
9 'Frost and Sun.' Year 1 children should be introduced to this game in stages, 'Frost' first. Teachers choose five children to be the catchers. The catchers chase the others and if they touch them the children touched have to stand still with their legs astride. The last five children to be touched, become the new catchers. Introduce the 'Sun'. The children who are standing with their legs astride can get back into the game if any child who is not caught crawls under their legs.

10 'Captain's coming.' The teacher explains that the children are to pretend to be sailors on a ship. The teacher is the ship's officer and gives commands and the children complete the task as quickly as possible.

   (i)   'Captain's coming!' All the children salute.
   (ii) 'Man overboard!' All the children lie down on the ground.
   (iii) 'Scrub the decks!' All the children kneel down and pretend to scrub the floor.
   (iv) 'Climb the mainbrace!' All the children pretend to climb.
   (v)   'Sharks!' The children lie down on their stomachs only.
   (vi) 'Starboard!' Everyone runs to the right of the area.
   (vii) 'Port!' Everyone runs to the left of the area.

During the playing of most of these introductory activities, the children will have been involved in 'simple competitive games, including how to play them as individuals, in pairs' and in a large group. They will have been 'involved in elements of games play that include running, chasing, dodging, avoiding and awareness of space and other players' (Department for Education and Employment 1995: 3). They will have therefore been beginning to learn aspects of the games area of activity in the Programme of Study for games in the National Curriculum.

Teachers must now concern themselves with teaching the children the other aspects of the Programme of Study, i.e., those concerned with learning games skills. The lesson structure for most lessons in Year 1 and Year 2 should be constructed with the following pattern.

Warm-up/introductory activity

This part of the lesson has two purposes:

• preparing the body for action;
• establishing the teacher's control, children listening to instructions.

Skill learning

• Learning specific techniques;
• application of the technique in a games-like situation;
• practice and repetition of technique or skill learned.

Game

• Game with whole class;
• game against self;
• game with /against a partner;
• game with a group/against another group.

Cool-down/concluding activity

Whole class activities which help the children to cool down and to calm down before returning to the classroom. Any equipment should be collected, properly stored and returned carefully to the storage area ready for use by the next class.

Observation of the children's performance is the key to their successful progress in games skill learning; it is a key teaching strategy in all Physical Education lessons. Teachers must therefore have a clear picture of each skill and how it should be performed if the children are to achieve their potential. The old adage that 'practice makes perfect' does not work when children are at the beginning of the process. It is essential, for instance, that children are shown the correct grip when holding a bat, the correct part of the foot to use when dribbling with a ball, and when to release the ball in various situations, e.g., when throwing and so on. Observation is coupled with assessment in games teaching. Teachers can assess the children's achievements as they observe them in action, can then identify any problems and give helpful feedback. They can use their assessments quite profitably to measure continuously the children's progress against the criteria listed in the Programme of Study. They can also use them as a basis for curriculum evaluation, and for reporting to parents.

To return to the teaching. After the warm-up or introduction to the lesson, teachers should choose whether or not to teach all the children a particular technique. This can be presented to them as a common task which they can all perform with differentiated outcomes. An example of this would be, for example, throwing a ball across the space for length. Teachers would teach the skill of underarm throwing and then let the children practise this skill at their own level of ability. Alternatively, they might want to focus on letting the children become 'ball happy', whereby several activities are introduced and the children try them. A teaching example of this might proceed as follows:

- 'Roll the ball over your body. Try up and down the front and back of your legs, between your legs, around your legs, around your waist, over your shoulder.'
- 'Run anywhere you like. On a signal, put your ball down and keep on running. On the next signal, pick up the nearest ball and keep on running.'

On the other hand, teachers might decide that various groups of children need to be given tasks with different levels of difficulty because of the developmental stage which they have reached. An example of this would be dribbling a large ball. Some children might not yet have achieved a satisfactory level when kicking a ball and so will not yet be ready to travel with it. Given this scenario, teachers would probably set up four different learning corners or stations where each child is offered activity tasks suitable for their learning stage; an example of activity stations is given below.

Station one

- Arrange four cones in a line, about 1 metre apart;
- each child has a size 4 ball and practises dribbling the ball with each foot around and between the cones;
- alternatively, set out five gates and let the children choose which ones to dribble their ball through.

Station two

- Each child has a hoop which is placed 2 metres from the starting position;
- each child has a ball and practises throwing the ball underarm to try and let it bounce inside the hoop.

Station three

- Two skittles are placed 2 metres apart, to form miniature goal posts;
- each child has a ball and a partner;
- each child has a turn at being the 'goalie' (receiving the ball) and a turn at kicking two balls in turn through the goal posts (sending the ball).

Station four

- Set out a number of cones, or skittles;
- each child has a ball and practises rolling it, aiming to hit the objects.

Teachers should move around the stations helping children who are having difficulty, also to give praise for achievement and progress, and to stimulate thinking and understanding by asking questions, for example, 'Which foot will you place in front of you if you want to throw the ball further? Where are you looking when you throw the ball? I wonder when you release the ball? Have you thought about moving your feet as the ball is released from your partner's foot?' Teachers can ask the children how they might alter the placement of the equipment to make the task harder/easier and can challenge the children with questions such as, 'Do you think you could do that faster?' or 'How many times can you hit the skittle?' or 'Can you dribble with your right foot as well as your left foot?' The same activity stations can be used for a number of lessons, before moving on to another set of activity stations with different skill practices, or to another method of working.

Skill learning with a partner is another valuable method which teachers can use to help children to make progress. Various skills can be learned and practised in this way: those that follow are listed in order of difficulty:

- run, skip, jump, hop around a partner (alternate turns with partner);
- follow a partner; copy whatever partner does;
- follow partner, listen for a signal and turn suddenly to change places;
- alternate foot tapping on top of a size 4 ball four times, then pushing the ball to partner;
- run around partner whilst holding a ball (any size and shape);
- roll a ball underarm to a partner (vary distance according to ability);
- bounce a size 4 ball to a partner (stand 2 metres apart);
- kick a large ball to a partner across a distance of 2 metres (vary distances),
- partner receives the ball with two hands;
- pass a large ball from right instep to left instep twice and then push the ball to partner;
- throw a size 4 ball up in the air, let it bounce once, partner catches it;
- partner holds a hoop in the air; practise throwing a size 4 ball through the hoop and running to catch it after it has bounced once;
- bounce a large ball into a hoop placed on the floor so that partner can catch it.

In all the above activities, teachers should encourage the children to use their left and their right feet and hands, and to co-operate with their partner. Teachers should teach all the skills to the children before they practise with a partner and should keep reinforcing the teaching points concerned with the position of their hands, feet and bodies, whilst watching the flight, or the pathway of the ball as it moves in their direction.

After the partner skills part of the lesson the children can then go on to play games, played with a partner, such as 'Crumbs and Crusts' or 'Butterfly touch'.

'Crumbs and Crusts'

The children line up in pairs standing at the side of their partner, one couple behind the other, and face the teacher. All the children in one line are named Crusts and the children in the other line are called Crumbs. If the teacher calls out 'Crumbs!' all the children in that line turn, and run to the side of the playing area nearest to them. Their partners turn and try and 'tig' them before they get there. If they are successful, they have won, if not, they have lost. The game begins again. If the teacher calls out 'Crusts', all the children in that line run as fast as they can to the nearest side of the playing area to them, before they are tagged by the Crumbs!

'Butterfly touch'

One line of children stand about fifteen strides away from their partners, and turn their backs on them. Each partner sets off from 'home' and creeps silently towards the back of their partner and gently touches them. They then turn and run 'home' as fast as they can. The children who have been touched must be quick to turn around and try and 'tig' their partner before they reach 'home'. If they can they have won. If they do not, they have lost.

The lesson can then come to a conclusion with a cool-down activity and the children can be taught how to collect and store the equipment.

During Year 2, most of the children will be reaching the stage when they are 'large ball happy', and will consequently have mastered most of the skills listed at the beginning of the chapter. They can now progress by being introduced to skill tasks and activities which include using one or more skills together, tasks such as:

- dribbling a ball with the instep of each foot, controlling it, turning in the opposite direction and continuing to dribble the ball without interrupting the flow of the movement;
- dribbling a size 4 ball around a partner, who tries to gain possession, and returning to start, and then kicking the ball to the partner if still in possession;
- bouncing a ball around partner, turning, and bouncing the ball to partner;
- using a soccer 'throw-in pass' to send the ball to partner, who receives it, picks it up and uses a throw-in pass to send it back;
- volleying a size 4 ball in the air – partner helps to keep the ball high;
- bouncing a size 4 ball to a partner, following the ball, running around partner and being in place to receive a ball which the partner sends;
- bouncing a large ball over a hoop or a skittle to a partner, and receiving the returning ball with two hands.

Also at the Year 2 stage, teachers should be able to observe that children have developed their manual dexterity sufficiently to be able to begin to work on motor activities associated with manipulating a small ball. If this is the case, then teachers should suggest that their children play with a small ball in any way they choose. Warm-up practices before lessons which concentrate on small ball work should always focus on activities which encourage manipulation of fingers, wrists and hands, in addition to those which are concerned with preparing the whole body for activity. The skill learning teaching which follows might proceed with small ball practices.

- 'Throw the ball high in the air, let it bounce and then catch it.'
- 'Throw the ball as far as you can, and run to collect it.'
- 'Bounce the ball under one leg, then the other. Can you bounce it whilst you walk along?'
- 'Can you throw the ball over your head from your right side to your left side and catch it with your left hand only? Can you throw the ball over your head and turn and catch it before it lands on the ground?'
- If a wall is available the children can practise throwing the ball against the wall and catching it after it has bounced on the ground once, then as it rebounds from the wall.
- If a wall is available, the children can practise throwing the ball underarm to hit various targets such as squares, triangles, circles and clock faces and enlarged dart boards with numbers to aim at. 'Which shape did you hit? What time is it on your clock? How many numbers have you hit? Which is your favourite?'
- Can you throw the ball under your leg to hit the wall? Can you bounce the ball between your legs to hit the wall and then catch the ball as it comes off the wall?
- 'Dribble the ball with a hockey stick: Can you move your ball so that it makes a square? A circle? How are you holding your stick? Which grip shall we use?'
- 'Hold your ball on a bat or racquet. Can you sit down without dropping it?'
- 'How are you holding your bat? Which grip shall we use?'
- 'Can you roll your ball around your bat without it dropping off?'
- 'Can you send the ball upwards from your bat and let it bounce back on it? How many times can you do it without dropping the ball?'
- 'Carry your ball on your racquet or bat. Can you hit it down on the ground and make it bounce? Can you walk along and do this?'
- Using a bat or a stick, A sends a small ball to B, who receives it, controls it, and sends it back to A.
- A, using a hockey stick, dribbles a small ball to B. B dribbles the ball into a space and A runs ahead of the direction of travel to collect it.
- 'Throw the ball underarm through hoops and rings.'
- 'Throw the ball overarm when sitting, then kneeling, then standing.'

After these types of practices, subsequent games played can involve the children in playing with their partner or competing against their partner. For example, a simple tennis-type game can be set up where, at first, Child A passes the ball on the racquet to Child B without dropping it. This can be followed by Child A dropping the ball off the racquet on to the floor near to Child B's feet. Child B then tries to scoop the ball up on to the racquet before tipping it off for Child A. The purpose in this game is to see how many times the children can exchange it without the ball rolling away. It is a game which involves co-operation from each child so that both can succeed.

An example of a game which is concerned with competing against another individual is as follows: each child has a hockey stick. Child A has a ball and dribbles it anywhere. Child B runs after Child A and tries to gain possession of the ball. Clearly the aim in this game is to compete against a partner for possession of the ball.

Teachers might also consider that the children are ready to use their new small ball sending skills to play a game of French cricket. Teachers can use the relay 'groups' for this game: one child has a cricket bat and defends his/her legs with it. One of the other three children is given a small soft ball. The aim of the game is to throw the ball so that it touches the batter's legs below the knee. Older children who play this traditional game are required to throw the ball from where the ball has landed, but children of this age can be offered the rule as follows: 'you may not throw from nearer than two strides away from the batter.'

It is usually at this stage in games lessons when children are heard to cry 'It's not fair!' and the real need for rules is understood! It would probably be appropriate at this stage, then, for teachers to share the concept of the need for rules with the children and ask them if they would like to suggest some other rules which would make the game more 'fair'.

At this stage, activity stations could be set up again for lessons following this series of practices. By doing this, each child can then make progress at his/her own rate and level of learning. After the activity station practices, the groups working in each area can then form teams which compete against each other to finish each lesson, or whole class games, such as the following, can be played.

The 'Numbers game'

Each activity group makes a circle and each child is given a number. Number 1 runs around the circle back to starting position, and touches Number 2 who runs around the circle, and touches Number 3, and so on, until all the children have had one turn each. The group which finishes first is the winner.

The 'Fishes game'

The whole class makes a circle. The children are given the names of three fish – cod, haddock, shrimp – alternately around the circle. If the teacher calls 'haddock!' every third child runs around the circle, and the first child to stand still having returned to their place is first home. Teachers can stimulate the children to run faster by suggesting that each 'haddock' tries to catch the 'haddock' in front! Teachers can add another dimension by calling out 'The tide's turning', at which point the 'haddocks' running around have to change direction and run the other way! Some teachers call out 'The sea is rough!' at which point all the 'haddocks' have to jump around the circle.

Another useful method to use to incorporate skill practices is to use the relay technique which the children probably learned in pre-school. Arrange the children in groups of not more than four people so that the general requirement for the children to be active is promoted. The relay formation which involves the children making a line one behind each other is adopted, and the children are given skill tasks to complete by their teachers. These skill tasks can be performed in a competitive atmosphere, but this does not necessarily mean that each group of children will compete against another. For instance, teachers might ask each group of children to count how many times they can complete the task before the teacher says stop. The children compete as a team against the clock, rather than against each other. Initially teachers can give the children tasks which are completed in the usual manner, i.e., each child takes a turn to complete the task and then returns to their own place in the relay team line. In subsequent lessons, practices can be set up where two children, for example, 1 + 2, face 3 + 4 . Child 2 kicks a ball to Child 3 and then runs to stand behind 4. Child 3 kicks the ball to Child 1 and then runs across to stand behind Child 1. Child 1 kicks the ball to Child 4 and runs to stand behind Child 2. Child 4 kicks the ball to Child 3 and runs to stand behind Child 3. Child 3 kicks the ball to Child 2 and runs to stand behind Child 1 and so on.

This formation, and this type of task, ensure that the children are active for most of the time, and have to practise a combination of skills. They have to combine the skill of kicking and following the ball, they have to be ready to receive the ball and they have to be aware of the space which they are working in. They also have to be aware of the movement of the other three players. The same formation can be used to practise throwing a size 4 ball or a rugby ball or hitting a small ball with a hockey stick and, eventually, if the children are skilful enough, hitting a small ball with a bat. Other suggestions:

- dribbling a large ball with the feet;
- dribbling a small ball with a hockey stick;
- bouncing a large ball.

At the end of lessons in which the children have been practising skill tasks in this manner, a good way to finish the activities is to have a competitive relay race. Ask the children for their ideas about the format, and any rules which they think should be applied. There is no doubt from observations of children taking part in relays that they enjoy them, provided that the teams are well balanced in terms of ability level, and that they are restricted to four members. In this situation, children have a good opportunity to be taught how to 'observe the conventions of fair play, honest competition, and good sporting behaviour as team members, how to cope with success and failure; to try hard to consolidate their performances'; and to 'be mindful of others and the environment' (Department for Education and Employment 1995: 2(2a, b, c, d).

Throughout all lessons teachers should keep a balance between 'high-level' activities and activities which are more static. In our climate, static activities can cause children to become cold, so teachers should feel confident about altering any planned lesson structure in order to warm the children up again. Children who become cold seldom enjoy games lessons! This might be an opportune time to teach children about 'the changes which occur in their bodies as they exercise' (Department for Education and Employment 1995: 3). For instance, they can be asked simple questions such as, 'What do you feel like?' 'Are you hot?' or, 'Is your face red?' 'Are you puffing?' Finally, 'I wonder why?'

The Programme of Study for games is straightforward and the End of Key Stage Descriptions are attainable by each child, provided that teachers follow a progressive scheme of work which gives every child the opportunity to have regular weekly lessons. Assessment in this area of activity will be mostly formative, and will be based on regular observations of the children as they work. Teachers should have decided as a whole staff which summative method of recording of achievement is to be used, and once again, it is worth remembering that there is no statutory requirement to assess their children's work in games, only a requirement to report to parents. Further information on planning, assessment and recording is offered in Chapter 7.

Chapter 6

Dance in Key Stage 1

People dance for many reasons. Some dance because it is part of a ritual, or to bring myths to life, or because dance is linked to a religious festival. Others dance because they are in love, or for the sheer pleasure of dancing, or because they see dance as a social activity. Some people need to dance for therapeutic reasons, whilst for many, dance has become a necessary 'nutrient' in their lives. People can dance who cannot talk, who cannot walk, who cannot see and who cannot hear. People can dance who have mental and emotional problems. Dance is a unique treasure which unites groups, which crosses the normal boundaries of colour, race, creed and intellect. Many people believe that there is a kinaesthetic sense which is embedded in our bodies, an aesthetic force, which dance experiences can liberate. Dance can have far-reaching effects on personality and on the concept of self, so that even children can be given an awareness of their bodies as a physical presence and an instrument of communication during dance lessons – an essential part of their education.

Throughout history dance has played an important part in the lives of people across the world and retains this place in most cultures today. In our own society, which has a continuously growing mix of people from different cultures, dance is valued for many reasons and by disparate groups. It is valued as a social and recreational activity, for its entertainment value, as a professional art form and as part of youth culture. Ziegler (1977: 3) has suggested that dance reflects 'the pulse of the nation', whilst Harlow and Rolfe (1992: 13) maintain that, 'it symbolizes everyday activity, and a means by which humans can interact and communicate'.

The joy of rhythmical activity is evident on any dance floor. It is evident at ceilidhs, and at folk dances, where the beat of the music is clear and the relationship with partners in the sets, plays an important part in the pleasurable experience. The same kinds of pleasure can be observed when boys take the lead in 'rap' and 'break dancing', working harmoniously together as they weave many intricate routines without interrupting the persuasive rhythmical beat of the music. But it is perhaps 'disco dancing' which can be classed as the dance of this generation, where toddlers gyrate along with brothers and sisters, and males and females of all ages share in a common pleasure which this activity has stimulated. Disco dancing can be performed anywhere; elaborate steps and patterns are not required. It is hardly surprising that we are all 'disco beat' conscious from a very early age. Babies arrive into the world having listened to the steady and rhythmical heartbeat of their mothers, and are soon surrounded by the beat of various sounds – the washer, the electric cleaner, the hairdryer, music of various types, and the rhythmical jingles and rhymes of child-hood. As soon as toddlers can sit, is it any wonder that they can be observed waving their arms rhythmically and when they begin to walk that they sway their bodies and jiggle their hips to any music or songs which they hear?

In educational settings, however, dance is seldom regarded as an important facet of daily life. In many schools, dance can only be regarded at best as a 'fringe' subject, hovering between the creative development area of learning in pre-school and the Physical Education Programme of Study in Key Stage 1. Unfortunately too, in recent times, the quality of dance teaching in primary schools has come under attack, having been regarded by various commentators as erratic or lacking in consistency. Dance has frequently been criticised as being non-existent in school programmes and has often been linked with poor teacher confidence in the teaching of the subject (Department of Education and Science 1978, Gulbenkian Foundation (Calouste) 1990, Cleave and Sharpe 1986, Williams 1989). It has also been suggested that teachers have not been convinced of its value in the school setting, perhaps because they have not felt competent to deal with dance or because they have been swept away by the tidal wave of guidelines offered to them in an attempt to improve their teaching performance.

It may be, of course, that this area of activity cannot be taught without an enthusiastic input from the teacher. As Harrison (1993: ii) argues in advising teachers, 'your own enthusiasm and involvement are essential to the children's success'. She also maintains that 'there is no single right way to introduce expressive actions to children', and, ironically, this could be where the confusion arises for primary school teachers when they attempt to teach dance, simply because the very essence of dance teaching lies in its individuality. Role models show competence, confidence, excitement, enthusiasm and a particular style of approach when they teach dance, which can seldom be copied. In addition, role models display as much diversity in their teaching styles as the dancers themselves. Consequently, the performance of these role models could forseeably have a negative effect on Key Stage 1 teachers, merely adding to their own feelings of inadequacy.

There is 'good news', however, in that SCAA does suggest that teachers should develop their own teaching style irrespective of 'role-modelling': 'No methodology is implied; it is a matter for teachers' professional judgement to decide the most effective and efficient way of teaching the National Curriculum' (ACAC and SCAA 1996: 9). Teachers also have much more control of the content of the curriculum than they perhaps realise. It may be that the advent of regular inspections has somewhat clouded some school's perceptions of their own entitlement to develop their own curriculum for their own children, but this is not the case:

> Decisions on the depth of treatment of aspects of subjects are also for the professional judgement of teachers. Not all aspects of the pro-grammes of study need to be taught in the same degree of depth or detail. It is also left to teachers to decide whether to include material from outside the programme of study in order to develop the school curriculum.
>
> (*ibid.*)

As far as the content of dance teaching is concerned, the dance area of activity in the Programme of Study sets out the knowledge, understanding and skills that should be taught to the children. It is a basic framework which should allow teachers to develop their own personal style of teaching and give them ownership of the content of the curriculum for their own children. The documentation gives the statutory information that pupils should be taught:

  a to develop control, co-ordination, balance, poise and elevation in the basic actions of travelling, jumping, turning, gesture and stillness;
  b to perform movements or patterns, including some from existing dance traditions;
  c to explore moods and feelings and to develop their response to music through dances, by using rhythmic responses and contrasts in speed, shape, direction and level.

(Department for Education and Employment 1995: 3)

The framework, then, is clear and easy to understand and should not create problems for teachers in relation to content. However, what may be difficult is to find strategies which can be employed to tease out the art form, to explore moods and feelings for each member in a class or to have the confidence to awaken the aesthetic force which undoubtedly exists in children. At a practical level it is also knowing how to summon up the enthusiasm which is needed to inspire 5-year-olds into aesthetic responses at 9 o'clock on Monday morning, or 6-year-olds at 2 o'clock on Friday afternoon! Such a scenario can be quite an unnerving consideration for many early years teachers. It certainly might be easier for teachers to choose to use the 'momentum of the moment', which pre-school teachers use as a strategy to enter the aesthetic area of dance activity – a strategy based on having been with the class all the time and perceiving that 'now could be a suitable moment' to awaken the aesthetic force, because the children are judged to be in a receptive mood. Unfortunately, the structure of timetables and the cohesion of programme planning (destructive elements in both arts teaching and arts learning!) often precludes the use of such a ploy. Often it is factors such as these which can cause unfair criticisms of Key Stage 1 teachers. It is very difficult to turn on both arts teaching and arts learning to order. The mood of the teacher and the children must be compatible for successful learning to take place and for any worthwhile contribution to the children's aesthetic development to be made.

As far as dance programmes themselves are concerned, it was suggested in Chapter 3 that a programme linked to cross-curricular learning, based on the topic or theme being explored in the classroom, was a possible method of taking 4-year-old children into the dance setting. Leese and Packer (1980) suggest that the holistic nature of primary school education can be complemented by dance. They argue that since one class teacher presents the entire curriculum to the same class and can see abilities develop, that class teacher can use this information to plan, assess and know where the children's needs lie. Dance can be a vital link in this interwoven, paedological chain. Whilst this method is well tried and to some extent successful in the teaching of dance for Year 1 and Year 2 children, it is nevertheless only one method of teaching dance which can be used. As children grow and develop emotionally, physically and intellectually, and become capable of higher-order skills and connections it is possible to offer other ways of dance teaching and learning. Dance teaching and dance experiences should never be put into a strait-jacket of tight structures and agreed formulas. If dance really is the aesthetic force which we believe it to be then many different teaching methods and planning structures should be investigated. The aim or objective might be quite different in one lesson compared to others, and some recognition of this should be built into any planning.

It would be quite wrong, however, to assume that dance was only concerned with aesthetics, because it can make important contributions to whole person development in other ways. Particular cognisance, for instance, should be taken of the contribution which dance plays in the development of healthy lifestyles. Research projects have shown that dance activities performed by primary school children out of school time contribute more to the children's health than any other activity which children become involved in (Sleap and Warburton 1992, Armstrong and McManus 1996: 30). It would also seem short-sighted to deny some flexibility being built into planning structures whereby teachers can respond to the interests of the children as and when these arise (Donaldson 1978). Sometimes, for instance, children might have a lesson or a series of lessons based on 'aerobics', a legitimate method of teaching dance, and one which undoubtedly fulfils some of the requirements of the dance area of activity listed in the Programme of Study, particularly the aspects concerned with developing control, co-ordination, balance, poise and elevation in the basic actions of jumping, turning and gesture, and the General Requirement of engaging in activities that develop cardiovascular health, muscular strength and endurance. As Titterton (1996: 21) has argued, 'sometimes aerobics performed to chart music is the only way to share initial dance experiences with resistant children in a class situation'. Folk dancing is another example of a different method of teaching dance which teachers can choose to use. Folk dancing gives teachers an opportunity to respond to the National Curriculum requirement to teach pupils to perform movements or patterns, including some from existing dance traditions. Additionally, like aerobic lessons, it gives children an opportunity to learn dance movements which are currently part of their own contemporary culture. It also gives them chances to explore moods and feelings. Dunn (1996: 5) comments,

> It must be fun! Sometimes children should be allowed to be less precise in their actions and be allowed to awaken social feelings, to laugh together, to giggle about missed steps together, to share a joke with their teacher. These are also 'moods and feelings' which should be explored.

Sometimes dance experiences can be shared with aspects of the music and drama curricula. There is no doubt for instance, that in some situations, children move more easily into dance through the medium of drama. Dramatic improvisation, role play and imaginative representation are closely allied to the creative and aesthetic aspects of dance for young children. Children can usually evoke a mood or feeling if they are given a concrete image to represent or to internalise. For example, children are much more likely to understand what teachers mean if they are asked to think about the story of 'The three little pigs' and to imagine how much strength would be needed to puff hard enough to blow a house down, than if they were simply asked 'to puff as hard as you can'. At this age, without a concrete context children are less likely to feel the same emotions or use as much effort for the action, than when they have listened to the story, discussed the underlying concepts and acted them out. The structured and guided development of imagery is essential to developing minds in the early years. All dance lessons do not have to be based on dramatic ideas, but for children, sometimes the arts are so closely woven together that it is important that there is no rigidity. Indeed it could be argued that it is impossible for teachers to know how children are creating the imagery. Sometimes, for example, if children are asked to move silently, smoothly and softly, one will tell you she is a thief, whilst another will say he is a swan, and another, a feather. Children seldom move without some association with a 'real' image which they have created in response to a movement directive at this stage in their learning. Some teachers in certain situations will suggest a concrete reference, for example, teachers might want the children to move with strong, direct, sharp movements and will suggest that a robot might move in this way. In this example one would expect that all the children will be creating the same images.

Similarly, the study of dance is inextricably linked to the study of music. The PE National Curriculum, for instance, clearly states that 'pupils should be taught to develop their responses to music through dances' (Department for Education and Employment 1995: 3) while the Music National Curriculum says that: 'pupils should be taught to respond to musical elements, and the changing character and mood of a piece of music by means of dance' (Department for Education and Employment (1995) *Music in the National Curriculum* London: HMSO, p. 5). Both the music and the Physical Education curriculum documentation also make reference to the need to teach pupils about the importance of rhythmic response and the repetition of patterns in the performance of both music and dance.

It could be argued, then, that the aesthetic forces of dance could be generated more successfully if some of the General Requirements outlined in the music curriculum were taken into the dance lessons, particularly the elements concerned with performing: 'When performing, composing, listening and appraising, pupils should be taught to listen with concentration, exploring, internalizing, e.g., hearing in their heads and recognizing the musical elements of: pitch, duration, dynamics, tempo, timbre, texture and structure' (Department for Education and Employment 1995: 2). Many dance teachers (Bruce 1988, Davies 1995, Fraser 1991, Slater 1993, Wetton 1995) believe that movement and sound should be considered together for effective dance teaching. Bruce (1988: 44) states that,

> Movement and sound make an exciting combination. We must consider the partnership both ways. Dancers find joy and enhancement in music as accompaniment and as a stimulus for their movement, and movement can be a vehicle for the comprehension and appreciation of music, especially for young children.

The use of voice sounds, body percussion, percussion instruments and all forms of recorded music are thus essential ingredients in dance teaching. Teachers should therefore consider the relationship between the two curriculum subjects when making planning decisions. To end with a particular example: disco dancing is the type of dancing which most children become involved in outside the environment of the school, yet they seldom have an opportunity to learn disco dancing in school. Educators seem frightened to allow this contemporary style of dancing to be explored, yet on the rare occasions that teachers use the disco format for a part of a lesson, children usually respond with energetic, enthusiastic and dynamic rhythmical movements which can seldom be drawn from them with such comprehensiveness when other music or other formats are offered. The question must be asked then as to why we deny children access to this form of dancing? Some children may value being taught how to disco dance so that they can be accepted socially, much as children like to be taught games in order to be accepted in playgrounds, so maybe the reasons for its exclusion should be re-examined.

There are many types of dancing which can be offered at Key Stage 1, and also many different teaching styles and methods which can be adopted. Various stimuli can be used to accompany the dancing, ranging from dramatic ideas to various types of accompaniment. Schools also have a plethora of choices available when planning for successful dance teaching and dance learning and can access many published guidelines when at the planning stage. There are plenty of LEA guidelines which have been prepared especially to help schools plan dance programmes. In addition, several authors have published books which are also useful for planning purposes and for school bookshelves. Harrison (1992) who was instrumental in teaching BBC dance programmes for schools for many sessions is inspirational in her approach. Her book 'Look! Look What I Can Do!' which contains useful guidance and much of the content of these programmes, has been a useful source of material for teachers for many years. 'Learning Through Dance' (Exiner and Lloyd 1987) is an invaluable guide for teachers seeking to integrate dance across the curriculum, whilst Davies and Sabin's book *Bodywork* (1995) is a practical teacher's resource book for primary dance and gymnastics, which serves the needs of non-specialists by providing a package which includes cross-curricular projects and offers a comprehensive range of activities and lesson plans linked to the whole school curriculum planning. Wetton (1995) in *Practical Guides: Physical Education* offers a sequential programme for dance across both Key Stage 1 and Key Stage 2, which is linked directly to the National Curriculum area of study for dance while Bunker, Hardy, Smith and Almond, (1994), Heath *et al.* (1994) and Lipscomb (1996) offer ideas and activities to fulfil the requirements of the National Curriculum in Key Stage 1. In addition there are many suggestions for lesson content in *Primary PE Focus*, the quarterly journal for primary school teachers. Harlow and Rolfe (1992), Davies (1995) and Bruce (1988) have published texts which will be useful and inspirational to curriculum leaders who require more information on the philosophy of dance, on planning and recording, on observation and on not only how to develop quality in children's dance, but how to ensure progression in their learning. Teachers might also like to consider showing children videos of dancers dancing. The TV companies often present materials which would assist children's conception of what is considered quality in dancing. The video of *River*

Dance, which shows both men and women dancing with sheer enjoyment, skill and exuberance, would be an example.

There are so many published texts and so many choices available to teachers that it becomes difficult to suggest a programme for dance at Key Stage 1. It could also be argued that a dance programme should not be planned in isolation, without any knowledge of the children for whom it is intended. The importance of knowing what children are interested in if learning is to take place has already been discussed. Also, there are some physical indicators of the children's developmental stage which need to be considered as forming the basis of the physical aspects of a dance curriculum. These are that:

- children are aware of where their feet, hands, faces, fingers and knees are, and can dance with these body parts easily;
- the children do not bring the middle of their bodies into movements, unless a specific body part is targeted;
- the children's balance is improving, and they can stretch high without wobbling, but can have difficulty in holding positions of stillness;
- bouncing and jumping, which need resilience in the legs and feet, is still not mature;
- most children can hop on each foot, on the spot and moving forwards;
- the children prefer quick movements;
- skipping has been acquired by 70 per cent of the children;
- quality in movements is beginning to develop;
- the children can create simple movement patterns if given guidance;
- the children find it easier to move to music rather than to dance rhythmically;
- the children are aware of the changes in music or stimuli and can change the movement response;
- awareness of the quality of the sound is developing in some children.

These physical characteristics could be linked to those 'qualitative' aspects of development which the children might possess in both movement and appreciation of sound stimuli, and together they could form the basis of a structure for planning the dance area of activity.

The dance movements which would also form part of this structure should include the following.

Awareness of the body
- Whole body movements concerned with opening and closing, twisting, rising and falling (focus on use of the head and spine);
- walk in the space, stop and turn around on the spot with arms stretched wide;
- run lightly in the space, hold arms out wide and turn around and around;

- shake every part of the body;
- flap arms in the space around the body, like a scarecrow;
- walk in time to the music, keeping very tall and narrow, like a lamppost;
- awareness of parts of the body: various movements of head, neck, shoulders, arms, fingers, wrists, waists, hips, legs, knees, ankles, feet, toes, eye lids, noses, ears, mouths, faces, bottoms, stomachs;
- symmetrical movements, simultaneous finger movement patterns, shoulders moving on identical pathways, elbow dances using symmetrical movements, pressing down with both feet at the same time, (sometimes with feet together, sometimes with feet apart); both arms moving on identical pathways and with identical speeds;
- leading the movements with specific parts of the body: elbows, bottoms, the little finger side of the hand;
- clapping hands, making a pattern, clapping different parts of the body;
- waving, saluting, fist-clenching, punching the air, fingers and toes – spreading and closing, wiping eyes, brushing hair;
- a body parts dance where different parts of the body meet and part;
- a dance where fingers and hands intertwine but never touch.

The body in stillness and motion

- Basic locomotor movements: walking, skipping, running, hopping, galloping, side-step slipping;
- basic locomotor movements finishing in complete stillness;
- twisting, curling and stretching, holding the finished position in stillness;
- two steps, followed by a position of stillness;
- dance created with moments of action and moments of stillness;
- sit, kneel and lie down, move non-supporting body parts to music or percussion and hold in stillness when the sound stops.

Travelling and jumping

- Basic locomotor movements on various pathways: straight, curved, circular;
- jumping on to two feet spread wide apart, long jumps and short jumps; jumping on to two feet which are close together, long jumps and short jumps; jumping patterns;
- stepping with alternate knees high, marching to music;
- leaping from one foot to another;
- bounce on the spot until the music stops, then hold the position;
- bounce shoulders, knees, toes, then leap forwards twice;
- leap in any direction and hold the shape in stillness;
- jump up from sitting, quickly, and jump along the floor.

Shape of the body

- Angular shapes, stretched shapes (both symmetric and asymmetric), curled shapes (try whilst standing, lying, kneeling, sitting);
- moving from one shape to another (slowly, quickly, smoothly, jerkily, lightly, strongly, directly, indirectly);
- twisted shapes held in stillness;
- hold left shoulder with right hand and right shoulder with left hand, make different arm shapes by moving elbows;
- curl up on the floor and make different body shapes by releasing one leg, or one arm or one leg and one arm, slowly or quickly, on straight or curved pathways.

Movement quality

- Press with both hands down onto the floor, stand up and press with both hands through the space. Pretend to be in a box and press out the sides to escape. Pretend to be inside a balloon and press against the inner surface (sustained, direct, firm movements);
- push both hands into the air, pretend you are pushing a heavy block of wood (sustained, strong, direct movements);
- pull in a fishing net (sustained, strong, direct movements);
- use slashing movements as if wielding a sword (sudden, strong, flexible movements);
- wring the water out of the washing (sustained, strong, flexible movements);
- dab the air. Pretend to dab the wall with paint (sudden, short, direct movements);
- the children pretend to flick the dust off themselves (sudden, light, flexible movements);
- stand with legs astride and push, pull and pummel a huge piece of dough (sustained, strong direct movements involving the whole torso).

Some words which could be used to conjure up the quality required in the actions and the mood to be established are listed below:

- clash, brittle, crack, crackle, crusty, jagged, craggy, rugged, clasp, grasp, freeze, sharp, icy, iceberg, spiky, spike, prickly, sudden, flash, knobbly, pop, burst, hook, rap, tap, knock, clap, bash, stark, flap, explode, clatter, bang, wallop, stamp, stomp, chop, jerk, hit, carve (strong, sharp, short direct movements);
- light, feathery, flimsy, gossamer, frothy, gently, float, softly, soundlessly, drift, flicker, simmer, fly (light, indirect movements);
- aggressive, strain, punch, pound, forceful, thunder, lightning, thrust, plunge, vibrate (strong, direct, sudden movements);

- slow, smoothly, creepy, crawly, calmly, smoky, wispy, sweep (soft, light, flexible movements);
- slither, screw (strong, indirect movements);
- swing, whip, slash, swish, swoop, saw (sudden, firm, strong, flexible movements);
- slice (sudden, firm, strong, direct movements);
- sway, rock, drift, wilt, billow, floppy, wobble, flutter, hover, waddle (soft, light, flexible, indirect movements);
- enfold, spread, unfold, surround, sink, fold, wrap (soft, light, indirect movements);
- flat, solid, tight, firm, compact, squat, pout, plug (short, strong, direct movements);
- sizzle, scurry, shrug, quiver, tremble (short, strong, indirect movements);
- motionless, numb, settle, frozen, still, rest, collapsed (various strengths, no movement).

Schools which choose to teach their dance programme of activity around cross-curricular themes have many choices. The following list gives some well-tried contexts:

- mini beasts;
- growing (frogs, tree shapes);
- water (stream, rivulet, river, ocean and underwater plants, creatures and shipwrecks);
- weather (spring, summer, autumn, winter; and snow and snowmen);
- journeys (magic carpet, air balloon, Christopher Columbus, Captain Cook, Scott of the Antarctic, Treasure Island, Jack and the Beanstalk);
- Knights of the Round Table;
- waxworks;
- clocks and timepieces;
- engines and robots;
- Enchanted Forest;
- toys (puppets, marionettes, mechanical toys, rag dolls, bendy toys, musical toys, Kelly doll);
- witches, wizards and sorcerers;
- 'Wind in the Willows';
- Snow White;
- 'Three Billy Goats Gruff';
- 'Three little pigs';
- festivals (5 November, fireworks, light, May Day, Chinese New Year, Chinese Kite Festival, coronations);
- the senses;
- the jungle;

- the North Pole;
- the desert;
- the rain forest.

Schools can also choose which sound stimuli to use to enrich the children's dancing, e.g., music, percussion, electronic sounds, recorded 'real' sounds (trains, sirens, animals, fireworks, water, winds, the sea, etc.) voice sounds, body sounds, words, rhymes, stories and poems. There are many pieces of music which have been used to accompany dance and which are still firm favourites of class teachers.

- 'Tijuana brass' (H. Alphert);
- *Pastoral Symphony* (L.V. Beethoven);
- *The Carnival of Animals* (C. Saint-Saëns);
- 'Circus polka' (I. Stravinski); *The Nutcracker* (P. I. Tchaikovsky);
- 'Radetzky-Marsch' (J. Strauss the elder);
- Dance of the tumblers' from *The Snow Maiden* (N.A. Rimsky-Korsakov);
- 'Danse macabre' (C. Saint-Saëns);
- *The Four Seasons* (A. Vivaldi);
- 'Fantasia on Greensleeves' (R. Vaughan Williams); 'Ritual fire dance' (M. de Falla);
- 'Claire de lune' from *Suite bergamasque* (C. Debussy);
- *Peer Gynt Suite* (E. Grieg).

There are also some more recent recordings of music which have become favourites in infant schools:

- 'The grasshopper's dance' (used in the TV milk bottle advertisement) (Bucalossi/ J. Hylton);
- 'Too many broken hearts' (J. Donovan);
- BBC sporting themes (various artists);
- *Sacred Spirit: Chants and Dances of Native Indians* (Virgin);
- 'The return of the gladiators' (Storm);
- *Now Dance: The Best of 1993 Disco Collection* (EMI Polygram);
- 'Chariots of fire' (Vangelis);
- 'Silent beauty' (Cross Culture);
- 'Elements' (Mike Oldfield);
- 'Rappin' with the ladies' (Shabba Ranks);
- 'Didgeridu' (Colour People);
- 'Essential' (Yello);
- 'Trance' (Europe Express);
- theme music from *The Lion King*;
- *Folk Dance* (BBC Enterprises).

Some teachers stimulate children into dance by the use of various props such as boxes, elastic, balloons, bubbles, scarves, cloaks, sticks and ribbons, whilst others use varying types of masks. All of these various stimuli have been shown to be effective in encouraging enjoyable dance experiences. They have also been found to be particularly useful as aids in helping children who have learning difficulties. Holding an 'object' seems to give added confidence to these children and when the music is played they can be observed to be 'outside themselves', presenting a different and more competent personality (Groves 1975: 5)

After considering the various types of stimuli which can be used to help children into dance, teachers will need to consider ways of structuring the dance lesson. A suggested way of working is outlined below – a lesson consisting of four discrete parts:

- warm-up;
- dance skill teaching;
- a dance experience;
- cool-down.

Warm-up

Warm-up periods should be concerned with preparing the body for the activities to be learned in the lesson. Teachers can choose whether to use taped music, percussion, body sounds or voice sounds for this part of the lesson. The warm-up part of the lesson should give the children an opportunity to use each part of their body in various ways and should help the children to increase their heartbeat and to extend their lungs. Four suggestions for a warm-up are outlined below.

Music

A suitable piece of music to use would be 'The grasshopper's dance' by Bucolossi and Hylton.

- Walk to the music;
- stand in one place and bend and stretch both arms in time to the music;
- tap each toe on the floor alternately;
- hop on one foot a few times, then the other foot;
- move each shoulder up and down alternately;
- move lower body from side to side;
- clench and open the fingers of both hands;
- bend the body from the waist and straighten up again;
- stretch both arms high in the air and then bend both elbows on to chests to the rhythm of the music;
- stretch both arms wide in any direction and on any plane and bend both arms back again;

- stretch high and then stretch low;
- walk around the area whilst bending from side to side;
- follow another person and keep in time to the music.

Body sounds

- Clap hands together, palms then backs of hands;
- clap each thigh with each hand;
- clap hands together whilst both arms are stretched high;
- clap hands together behind backs;
- stretch each arm on any level or plane then bring the hands together to make a loud clap;
- clap high in the air, then clap low to the ground;
- clap both hands out to the left side of the body, then to the right side;
- clap hands behind each knee in turn whilst lifting one leg;
- make shuffling noises on the floor by dragging each foot across its surface;
- stand with legs astride and drag the left foot across the floor to touch the right foot and back again, then repeat with the right foot across to the left foot;
- stamp each foot in turn, then try and stamp both feet together;
- stamp around the area making as much noise as possible then change to shuffling;
- run making a lot of noise, then run without making any noise;
- make three noisy jumps, then three quiet resilient jumps.

Percussion

- Walk, skip, stride and jog to the various beats of a drum;
- shake hands, feet, legs and arms in turn and then the whole body to the sound of a tambourine;
- change movements in response to the sounds and the rhythms created by the teacher, for example, steady beats on the drum;
- quick, shaking sounds of the tambourine, quick beats on the drum, slow scratching sounds on the skin of the tambourine.

Language

- Stretch, jump, stretch, jump, jump, jump, jump;
- twist and hold;
- stretch and hold, punch, punch, punch;
- whip and freeze;
- knock (each knee one against the other, on an imaginary door, elbows together);

- wobble, wobble, wobble;
- flutter;
- sway;
- rock;
- crawl, scurry, slither;
- spiky and freeze;
- sink and collapse;
- sway, wobble and sink;
- bounce, bounce, bounce and turn;
- stretch and sink;
- pop! pop!

Dance skill teaching

This second part of the lesson should be used to provide an environment where the children can have an opportunity to learn new dance techniques and to explore moods and feelings. The content should prepare the children for the dance experience which will follow.

One example for a dance skill sequence is given below, themed around clocks (clockwork and electronic) and mechanical toys.

Teachers should have talked to the children about clocks and mechanical toys in the classroom during classroom work on the theme so that they have had an opportunity to think about clocks and mechanical toys and how they work. Thus, an introduction to various dance movements might begin by asking the children 'Do you remember when we were talking about clocks?' The teacher might then continue:

'What did the clockwork clock sound like? Move your heads from side to side as I say tick! tock! Try and use the same amount of energy for each movement so that you make a rhythmical pattern.'

Teachers could use a metronome for these actions so that the children can see the pendulum working and match their movements to the arm of the metronome.

'Stand with your left arm stretched down at the side of your body and the other arm stretched out wide from your shoulder. Bring your left arm up so that it is stretched out wide, as you smack your right arm down to your side. Begin a clockwork movement as I say tick! tock! Let each arm move, one up and one down, on tick and then on tock.'

Teachers should emphasise the need for the children to keep their bodies still, and to keep each arm stretched. Teachers can help the children to feel the sharp, short, clockwork rhythm by the manner in which they modulate their voices as they say tick! tock!

'Which other parts of your body could you use to make a tick-tock rhythm?' This could be:

- short, sharp movements from right to left with each hand, then with both hands;
- with two knees from side;
- with one finger;
- with each foot;
- bend elbows and let hands swing from side to side;
- rocking from side to side from the waist;
- bending from the waist, downwards and then back to standing;
- stepping on to one foot on 'tick' and to the other on 'tock'.

Teachers should encourage the children to try this action stepping from side to side and then with one foot in front of the other. Older infants could be encouraged to make head and then whole body movements as they step.

'Which other kind of clock did we listen to? (the electronic clock). What sound did it make?' (short rhythmic bleeps). What kind of movements should we make? (short, sharp, sudden movements). Some suggestions would be:

- one finger poking out and bending in;
- all the fingers on one hand stretching out suddenly from a clenched fist then a sudden re-clenching of the fingers;
- all fingers and both hands;
- bending knees and straightening knees;
- tapping each foot on the floor with sudden, short, sharp movements.

The theme concerned with clocks can be developed further in the next lesson and then teachers can link the concept of clockworkings and electronics in later lessons when the emphasis can be placed on mechanical toys.

The dance experience

In this part of the lesson the children should be given a framework for a dance experience which includes some of the movements practised above.

Teachers should allow some freedom for the children to interpret the framework with their own choice of movement. An example is suggested below:

'Electronic and clockwork clocks help us to wake up in the morning. Can you remember what the alarm sounded like? It surprised us. Curl up small and when you hear the alarm, shoot your hands in the air twice, then when you hear the next two rings, jump up. On the next sounds move from foot to foot. Remember to make short, sharp, sudden movements, and surprise me! Remember to be still when the alarm is not making a sound, and be ready to move again when you hear the alarm again.'

Older infants can be encouraged to make a rhythmical dance pattern based on the sound pattern of electronic alarms (chimes, fanfares, soft bells, church bells and in response to the number of rings or bleeps). Teachers can suggest a framework and then give the children an opportunity to create their own pattern. As the theme develops in later lessons, teachers can give their children dance experiences based on different types and sizes of clocks, clockwork toys, clockwork trains, robotic figures and so on.

Cool-down

This part of the lesson should be used to calm the children both physically and emotionally in readiness for re-entry into the classroom. Various methods can be used. Teachers could play a piece of recorded music to calm the children, for example, 'Adagio for strings'. (Samuel Barber), and ask them to sit down and listen carefully to the music. Teachers could encourage the children to stretch their arms slowly and smoothly as the music plays, then to move their upper bodies as they move their arms. The children should be encouraged to make soft, smooth, flexible, curved or spiralling movements with their limbs and bodies. The children could walk slowly and smoothly (like a king or queen with a crown on their head?) around the hall and finally leave the hall as the music continues to be played.

Teachers could use their own voice to calm the children. Teachers should use a soft voice or a whisper to ask the children to lie down and stretch out on the floor. The children should be asked to stretch out each limb in turn and stretch it as far as possible. (Teachers can check the children's faces to see if they are making the required effort!) Teachers should then use the softest whisper to ask the children to spiral upwards like a wisp of smoke, to feel light and soft until they are in a place where they can hold a curved shape in stillness. The children who are listening carefully will hear the direction to go back to the classroom without a sound!

Percussion can be used to give the children a contrast to a lesson which has been concerned with sharp, short movements, for example, use a set of bells to create a soft tinkling sound. Let the children move their fingers around their own bodies, high in the air, behind their backs, at the sides of their bodies, in and out of each leg and then freely choosing where they would like to move. Teachers should try to create a calm and soft atmosphere by keeping the sound low throughout.

Each of the themes suggested above can be developed in this manner, but it must be emphasised that teachers should feel that they can contribute their own ideas to the content rather than feeling that they must follow a published scheme of work. Dance lessons are much more meaningful if the children's immediate interests are absorbed into the lesson content.

Another type of dancing which teachers offer to children as part of the National Curriculum is folk dancing performed to recorded music. The choice of music which can be used for folk dance lessons is wide and varied. There are several sources from which teachers can buy, e.g., BBC Educational Enterprises have a collection of five cassettes (and ten lesson notes) which form the basis of a ten-week folk dance programme)see resources section). The music on the cassettes has been specially arranged and played in a contemporary style based on traditional British folk music. The music, played by Dingles, a folk dance band, is a blend of traditional and new tunes, arranged and played in a traditional style, but brought up to date. Another source of music is contemporary 'chart music', e.g., 'Too many broken hearts', sung by Jason Donavan. This piece has a thirty-two-bar tune which can be broken down into eight or sixteen-bar phrases and gives teachers and children an opportunity to use the music to create their own dances, using traditional folk dance steps and formations. However, the most well-known source for information about music for folk dancing is the English Folk Dancing and Song Society, which has a comprehensive ` catalogue providing a list of resources for dance which, in addition to music, includes books and booklets which will be helpful for teachers (see resources section). Dunn (1996) has also produced a booklet which teachers will find very useful. This booklet contains many fun ideas with which to start each lesson and to help children into the dance. It offers a useful compendium of information on folk dance steps and formations and several dances which the author has enjoyed with his own classes of children for over ten years. Wetton (1996) also offers some suggestions for folk dance lessons in the book *PE: Practical Guides for Teachers*.

The structure of a folk dance lesson is similar to the structure for any dance lesson. As is the case in all Physical Education lessons it is important to have a warm-up period. In a folk dance lesson, however, there should be an additional emphasis on helping the children to move with the music. In fact, some teachers choose to use the music for the warm-up which they will eventually use throughout, so that the children can dance freely to it at the beginning and become familiar with the tune. By doing this, teachers believe that the children will learn to recognise the musical elements in the piece such as pitch, duration, dynamics, tempo, texture, timbre and structure, and especially the rhythm. On the other hand, some teachers prefer to offer children a variety of different pieces of music for each part of the lesson, whilst other teachers encourage children to bring their own choice to the lesson, music which might be 'rap' or 'disco', which will give an added flavour to the proceedings. The important thing to remember here is that whatever the choice of music, the idea is to 'get them going!' i.e., to give the children selections which are literally 'music' to their ears, so that they feel they want to dance and enjoy the activity.

A four-part structure is recommended as a format for folk dance lessons, starting with a warm-up, followed by an introduction to folk dance steps and conventions, and concluding with a dance experience and finally a cool-down.

Warm-up

For the warm-up, let the children clap to the tune, stamp their feet on the spot, and walk, skip or jog around the room, in an effort to keep in time with the music. Suggest that they move their shoulders and hips and feel the rhythm throughout their whole body. They should be given the opportunity to feel free in their movements and should also be given a chance to be exuberant and expressive so that a 'feel-good' factor begins to emerge because of the activity. Older infants who have had earlier experiences of folk dance lessons should be given the opportunity to choose the type of movement which they think fits the music of the day rather than being given a framework of ideas by the teacher.

Introduction to folk dance steps and conventions

The second part of the lesson should then be concerned with introducing the children to some of the steps and conventions of the traditional style of folk dancing without losing the enjoyment factor, an essential ingredient of social dancing. In the earliest lessons, simple steps and formations should be presented so that the children begin to listen for the beat of the music. Let them walk or skip around the room, then suggest that they stop and listen to the music occasionally before continuing to move. Teachers should make the children aware of different directions, particularly 'face me', 'towards me', 'this way' and 'that way'. Eventually they will need to follow instructions when dances are being constructed, so they will need some practice in identifying body parts. A fun method of learning this would be to recall the nursery song, 'One finger, one thumb, keep moving'. Another fun game would be to let them skip around the room and when the music stops, call out a part of the body which they should wiggle.

Eventually it will be possible to offer more specific folk dance activities such as walking or skipping around the room and stopping from time to time to shake hands, or link elbows with other children. Playing 'Follow my leader' would be another fun activity. The children could follow the teacher at first and then take turns to be the leader of a small line of children themselves. They could also make groups of four and take turns to skip around the other three children. Bring in the convention of arches by letting six children make three arches for the other children to skip under. Patterns are important in traditional folk dancing. Early patterning can be introduced by asking the children to trace foot patterns of numbers or letters on the floor with their toes.

As the children develop their listening skills and their ability to move in time to the music they can be introduced to more complicated skills such as galloping, or side-step slipping, the running step or the springing walking step. All these new skills should be introduced slowly, so that the children do not 'fail' in their attempts. The dancers should also be introduced to working with a partner (who need not be of the opposite sex).

Partner skills include:

- walking towards each other and backwards from each other;
- linking elbows and turning around with each other on the spot (using right and then left arms);
- facing each other, join hands with stretched arms and turn once clockwise (the two-handed turn);
- shaking right hands and left hands at the same time, then holding the position whilst turning around (swinging);
- face partners, walk a few steps to pass right shoulders, then backs, then left shoulders and finish facing again (do-si-do);
- walking alongside a partner whilst walking forwards and backwards;
- facing a partner and taking turns to side-slip, step to the right and then to the left to return to original place;
- join right hands and turn on the spot (right-hand turn).

Dance experience

The third part of the lesson should focus on giving the children a dance experience. In the first two lessons, the children can play traditional party games such as 'musical statues', 'musical mats' or 'musical bumps'. These will probably be known to the children and should build their confidence. They will need to listen to the music in these games so that whilst they are having fun they will also be learning an important music and dance skill. The next step would be to introduce some phrasing into the activities. Most folk dance music is written on a sixteen-beat (eight-bar) phrase. Teachers should give their children some activities where they can begin to hear the changes in the music or count the number of beats. Try clapping with the children for sixteen beats, then tapping heads for sixteen beats, clapping hands for sixteen beats then tapping heads for sixteen beats. The children do not need to count, they just need to follow the teacher. Another experience would be to try walking in the room for sixteen beats, then standing still for sixteen beats and so on.

The children will probably have played circle games whilst in pre-school, so the next step could be to make up a circle dance. For example: join hands in a circle. Walk to the left for fifteen steps (use one step to change direction) then walk to the right for fifteen steps. Drop hands and face into the centre of the circle. Walk into the middle for seven steps, use one step to adjust balance, and walk backwards back to the starting position for eight steps. Clap own hands sixteen times, and then heads sixteen times. Keep repeating the dance until the children are happy with the formation of the dance and then they can skip instead of walking. Teachers and children can continue to make up their own dances, basing them on eight-bar phrases.

Soon it will be possible to introduce the children to some of the traditional folk dances. The following dances are ones which infant children are known to enjoy:

circle dances: 'Circassian circle'; 'the Jolly Roger';
double circle dances: 'Pat-a-cake polka';
longways dances: 'The Oxo reel'; 'Brighton Camp'; 'the Virginia reel'.

The Programme of Study for dance in the National Curriculum states that children should be taught movements or patterns, including some from existing dance traditions, and so it is important to note therefore, that whilst English folk dancing is offered as an example in this text, other dance traditions should not be excluded where they could add to the richness of a dance programme.

Cool-down

Teachers can choose whether to use music, voice sounds, words, poetry or percussion to accompany the children's movements. The accompaniment should consist of quiet sounds so that the children's bodies are brought back to normal functioning. Several ideas are offered below:

- ask the children to use the tip of their right finger to trace large circles, squares and triangles in the air. A suitable piece of music to use would be 'Clair de Lune' by C. Debussy;
- the teacher can face the class and ask them to copy her slow sustained movements in silence;
- if the lesson has been concerned with dramatic imagery, a suitable poem or an extract from a story could be read to children. The piece should convey a quiet mood and evoke slow and sustained movements;
- after a folk dance lesson the children might enjoy cooling down by

clapping out a rhythm to a well-known poem such as 'A sailor went to sea, sea, sea, to see what he could see, see, see. And all that he could see, see, see, was the bottom of the deep blue sea, sea, sea' (Smith 1982: 53).

Chapter 7

Planning and organisation
Planning the curriculum

The foundation for planning the PE curriculum in the early years is located in the the Programme of Study in the National Curriculum and states that:

> In each year of the key stage, pupils should be taught three areas of activity: Games, Gymnastic Activities and Dance, using indoor and outdoor environments where appropriate. In addition, schools may choose to teach Swimming in Key Stage 1 using the programme of study set out in Key Stage 2.
>
> Throughout the key stage, pupils should be taught:
>
> * the changes that occur to their bodies as they exercise;
> * to recognise the short-term effects of exercise on the body.

(Department for Education and Employment 1995: 3)

The details of the documentation in relation to each of the three activity areas within the Programme of Study specify what children should be taught in terms of content in these three activity areas. The National Curriculum documentation also lists thirteen General Requirements which should apply to the teaching of Physical Education across all key stages. These thirteen requirements are grouped under three main headings: (1) the promotion of healthy lifestyles; (2) the development of positive attitudes; and (3) ensuring safe practice. In the chapters specifically related to the teaching of the three activity areas within the Programme of Study, some suggestions on how to achieve each of the General Requirements and some suggestions for the curriculum content have been included. However, schools are able to make their own choices about the formation and planning of their own Physical Education curriculum and the methods which they will use to ensure that both the content of the Programme of Study and the General Requirements are included. Schools can also feel confident in formulating, organising and evaluating their own Physical Education curriculum based on the educational objectives which the staff in each school consider should be the Physical Education part of each school's whole school curriculum.

In order to facilitate this planning, some schools appoint curriculum co-ordinators to take the responsibility of drawing up a balanced curriculum. It is the co-ordinator's task to ensure that the curriculum is well planned and well resourced and, in some cases, take the responsibility for ensuring that what is planned is taught and evaluated. In order to be successful at this task, co-ordinators have to ask themselves fundamental questions, or, where the task is shared by the whole staff, introduce the relevant questions to stimulate discussion. Often this kind of debate can be developed as an INSET activity.

Tyler (1947: 1) suggests that there are four fundamental questions which should be answered in developing any curriculum and plan of instruction, and which might lead to a curriculum model. These are:

- What educational purposes should the school seek to attain?
- What educational experiences can be provided that are likely to attain these purposes?
- How can these educational experiences be effectively organised?
- How can we determine whether these purposes are being attained?

Nevertheless, it would seem that any discussion about the purposes of Physical Education lessons should begin with a discussion of the learners as a source of educational objectives. Following this, it would appear to be important to consider suggestions about objectives from subject special-ists and then go on to consider the use of the philosophy and the psychology of learning in an attempt to select objectives. Finally, agreed objectives should be presented in a form which will be helpful in selecting learning experiences for the learners and also in guiding teachers towards achieving them.

THE LEARNERS

When children enter Key Stage 1, they move from being offered a pre-school curriculum, based on child development, to a curriculum which is subject-focused. Before entering statutory schooling, a large part of their pre-school day will have been concerned with learning by doing, but on entering school at 5, the change is made to a curriculum focused around the core subjects of the National Curriculum, the result of which for many children means considerable change. Children do not develop at the same rate as each other physically, as Tanner's research (1978) has indicated. He has shown that there are wide variations in the growth patterns of children and offers ample evidence which should persuade teachers of the import-ance of a continuous focus on physical activities as a learning medium throughout the early years in school. Many early years specialists are well aware of these facts and so it is difficult to understand why so many schools reduce the children's physical experiences in the classroom and limit Physical Education lessons to two 20-minute periods each week. Some children are not yet ready to take on the rigours of a curriculum where movement opportunities are limited, since many do not yet have the physical skills with which to cope with an academic day focused on fine motor activities consisting of refined eye–hand co-ordination skills. It should also be remembered, too, that children's knowledge, including their knowledge of maths, science and language, has been located until now in active participation with the real world. Donaldson (1978), in discussing why children find school learning difficult when they enter statutory schooling, argues that children's knowledge of language is embedded in the events which accompany it, and so they are more concerned to make sense of what people do, when they talk, rather than to decide what the words mean. It would seem to follow then that when children come into school, having learned much of what they know from using their bodies, that the change to a less movement-oriented curriculum can be disorientating in its effect, unless teachers are sympathetic to their needs. These physical needs must be recognised as the children develop from outward thinkers reacting to the real world, to learners and thinkers who can, as Donaldson suggests, turn language and thought in upon themselves and become able to direct their own thought processes. As researchers have shown us too, many children, in addition to needing sympathetic care, have particular problems associated with motor capability which need attention throughout the time that they are in primary school. For these children in particular it is very important to acquire some of the fundamental skills expected of them in the core curriculum subjects through a well-balanced and regular physical education programme.

Those who teach early learners know how much all young children are motivated to take part in Physical Education lessons and it does not take a highly intelligent person to explain why this is the case. Children are motivated to take part because the subject is one which they know most about. It is located in physical action, a medium which they have been using since birth to learn about the people and objects in their world. It is very surprising, therefore, that teachers do not make more use of Physical Education lessons as a means of helping children to acquire knowledge in the early years.

Education is knowing how children are developing so that knowledge can be assimilated in enjoyable ways. As will be shown later, children in the age group 4–8 are in a life phase where they are developing all the motor skills and patterns which they will ever learn, and to deny them access to activity is to deny them the fundamental right to learn the skills which will allow them to succeed in life.

SUGGESTIONS ABOUT OBJECTIVES FROM SUBJECT SPECIALISTS

The General Requirements for PE in the National Curriculum, which were formulated by a group of Physical Education and sports specialists, should be applied to the teaching of Physical Education. However, staff in schools have the right to make judgements about the balance of the PE curriculum in their own schools if they believe that to do so would be of benefit to their own children. Clearly staff will be more effective in making judgements about the objectives which they want to achieve if they base these judgements both on good sound knowledge and information about the curriculum area and the children whom they teach. There is a good deal of advice available from specialist physical educationists about formulating objectives and what these objectives should be. Alderson and Crutchley (1990: 55), for example, argue that the objective in the early years (4–7) is about mastery in movement. They suggest that these years are 'comprised of gaining basic efficiency in a range of movement–skill categories which will provide the necessary foundation for later involvement in sport'. Gallahue (1989) asserts that the period from 2–7 years of age is the time when the basic motor skills and patterns are developed, and suggests that the objective in the early years should be to ensure that all children are given an opportunity to develop these skills and patterns. Sugden (1990), in stating that children will develop all the fundamental skills they will ever possess by the time they are 7, considers that one of the most important objectives in Key Stage 1 is to ensure that children learn all the fundamental physical skills during this time. As far as motivation is concerned, Fox (1994) argues that children of this age are well motivated to take part in Physical Education lessons and that because of this, it is 'a profitable time to develop their repertoire of physical skills'. Fox agrees with Alderson and Crutchley, that one objective to aim for in pupils' early years is 'to establish a dynamic foundation to their physical selves, so that they feel they are equipped to take up the physical challenges of more formal sports and activities that lie ahead' (ibid.: 16). Fox also explores the notion that involvement in PE will have the effect of developing pupils' self-esteem, although he does draw our attention to research evidence offered by Harter (1985, 1986) that for children in the age group 5–8 years, self-esteem does not exist as a concept. Corbin (1989), however, states that what does exist, for those children who have experienced a supportive upbringing, is a feeling of unquestioned self-worth. My view would be that one of the most important objectives for teachers in Physical Education lessons would be to develop this same self-worth in all children. This is a view commonly held by early years specialists, who believe that developing a feeling of self-worth in children is an objective which should permeate the whole early years curriculum.

In the early part of this century, it was believed that an important objective for pupils to gain from Physical Education (particularly games playing), was 'character building'. There are still echoes of this in the detail of the General Requirements in the National Curriculum, where in the section on developing positive attitudes, a statement is made that 'pupils should be taught to observe the conventions of fair play, honest competition and good sporting behaviour' (Department for Education and Employment 1995: 2(2a)). In Key Stage 1, however, these objectives can be translated into conventions concerned more with learning how to share equipment, how to take turns and how to play with others, particularly in the playground and out of school situations, since most educationalists would see them as social skills. These social skills can be learned through involvement in Physical Education lessons, particularly when the children are given an opportunity to be guided into acceptable play conventions with their teacher on the school playground. Developing social skills, then, is an important objective which should be included in the curriculum.

The Physical Education Association of the United Kingdom, showed in a survey in 1987 that teachers placed self-realisation as one of the three top priorities in their objectives for pupils taking part in PE lessons. Also, as Fox reports (1992: 34), the teachers regularly included as important objectives 'related psychological constructs such as moral development, social competence and emotional stability'. Many researchers (Sleap and Warburton 1992, Armstrong and Biddle 1992,) emphasise the need to ensure that an objective of the curriculum should be to establish good attitudes towards physical activity in the early years in order that children develop lifestyle patterns of activity which will lead to the prevention of heart disease in later life.

Another important objective in developing positive attitudes to activity is to prevent the onset of obesity in children by the provision of a physical education curriculum where children can be active for most of the time. Dr M. Wiseman, Chief Nutritionist at the Department of Health (1995) reported on a survey of children aged 5–11, which indicates that British children overall are becoming fatter and heavier. The National Nutrition and Physical Activity Task Force have met recently (1996) to formulate a strategy to help people to prevent this increase in weight and its associated health problems; curriculum co-ordinators should bear this in mind.

In conclusion, most specialists would assert that the most important objective of all, if all the objectives which are outlined above are to be fulfilled, is to make children's early experiences in Physical Education lessons enjoyable. There can be little doubt that enjoyment of Physical Education lessons will foster both immediate and future participation (Armstrong 1990, Chadzoy 1996, Cooper 1995, Dunn 1996, Fox 1992, Jones 1996, Sleap 1988, Warburton 1995, Wetton 1995, Williams 1989).

THE USE OF PHILOSOPHY IN SELECTING OBJECTIVES

Most schools in Great Britain normally have a whole school policy which frequently reflects the democratic society in which they exist.There is no question that all schools will be influenced by the values which exist in contemporary society and particularly those values which the government places on the education system. As far as PE is concerned, the government has recently become involved in a 'Sport debate' (Department of National Heritage 1995: 2) which includes 'a commitment to putting sport at the heart of weekly life in school, and to re-establishing sport as one of the great pillars of education alongside the academic, the vocational and the moral' (John Major). In the document *Sport: Raising the Game: The First Year Report* (Department of National Heritage 1996), the Minister for Sport, Iain Sproat, outlines the progress which has been made in fulfilling the Prime Minister's 1995 agenda. The values which the Prime Minister believes to be important are highlighted throughout this document, in which the Minister for Sport revisits the thirty-eight action points which were set out in the 'Sport debate' report. There are eight action points which serve as future indicators for school PE curricula. The headings to the eight action points concerning schools specifically read thus:

1 Revised Physical Education (PE) curriculum comes into effect in August 1995 with an enhanced role for team games.
2 Working group to examine best practice in the teaching of sporting conduct.
3 All schools should offer two hours per week of PE and Sport in formal lessons.
4 School annual reports and prospectuses will set out sporting provision.
5 A new sportsmark scheme will recognise the best schools with additional Gold Star awards for the most innovative (primary schools in 1997/8).
6 OFSTED will inspect quality and range of games offered as part of the PE curriculum and report on this and on provision outside the formal curriculum.
7 OFSTED to conduct a survey of the state of school sport to identify good practice.
8 Chief Inspector to report annually on the state of PE and Sport in schools.

(Department of National Heritage 1996: 2–5)

In the light of these pronouncements, most Physical Education specialists are of the opinion that the government is anxious to raise the standard of sport in this country and applaud it for its efforts. There are those, however, who are unhappy with the thrust of the action agenda, which seems to be centred around team games, even to the extent of including the necessity for pupils in Key Stage 1 to be involved in competitive games. The concern is over the notion of 'competition'. Many specialists are unhappy about this because they know, for instance, that for many pupils, an active life is generated, not necessarily through competition, but through dance, or swimming or gymnastics, and that for most it is the health and well-being aspects of PE which are motivating and pleasurable. I am of the opinion that had the report restricted the use of the term 'sport' (which can be defined as 'an individual or group activity pursued for exercise or leisure often in a competitive form', Collins 1990: 40) and not pressed so insistently for the emphasis on team games, specialists would have been more sympathetic towards this action agenda. Such an interpretation of the term 'sport' would have allowed specialists and teachers in schools to focus on a more balanced curriculum, which would permit all children's interests to be nurtured.

Nevertheless, those of us who enjoyed team games when we were pupils can understand why the government is pressing for a commitment to team games. Most of us appreciate that through an involvement in team games we learned essential leadership skills, the value of competition, how to win and lose with constraint, the value of being part of a team, of encouraging and supporting weaker players, of striving for excellence and the wonderful camaraderie of 'team' which has lasting social benefits and the feeling of belonging. But then, as now, many other pupils prefer to take other forms of exercise and pursue other worthwhile and satisfying forms of physical activity. Undoubtedly, there is a place for introducing competition through involvement in games activities in the early years Physical Education curriculum but there should also be an equal place for gymnastics and dance, particularly if all children's needs are to be satisfied and all the physical, social, emotional, educational and health objectives are to be realised.

OBJECTIVES ASSOCIATED WITH THE PSYCHOLOGY OF LEARNING

Since educational objectives are the results to be achieved from learning, it follows that a knowledge of how young children learn can be helpful in ensuring that the objectives are realised. A knowledge of the psychology of learning will undoubtedly help teachers to distinguish changes in pupils that can be expected from a learning process and those which cannot. For instance, at a basic level, teachers know that pupils' social behaviour can be guided into acceptable levels by placing them in a learning process in games playing situations. On the other hand, however, whilst it is possible for children to acquire knowledge about health and to develop good health habits from a learning process concerned with knowledge of the impact of exercise on the body, it is clearly impossible for them to gain an increase in height because of involvement in this learning process. Equally, some educational objectives which might have been seductive to curriculum planners, such as expecting pupils in the early years to sit still all day without talking, are not possible to achieve. At a different level, a knowledge of the psychology of learning enables teachers to know at what age various objectives could be attainable. Very few educationists would agree that there is one age level when a particular skill can be most effectively learned, but a knowledge of the psychology of learning can give teachers some indicators about when pupils are ready to learn, a suitable sequence of learning and the probable length of time which will be needed for a pupil to achieve the desired knowledge. For instance, pupils in Key Stage 1 cannot be expected to play team games, since in order to do this they would need to have acquired many games skills which, as learning theory shows us, would have been impossible for pupils to achieve during their lifespan so far. Nor would it be possible to place early years pupils in a situation where they were expected to play a team game, because it would cause almost all children to fail and therefore to lose their motivation to learn.

Tyler states that one of the most important psychological findings for curriculum planners is that most learning has multiple outcomes. In PE, an example of this would be in a games lesson where the teacher asks the child to collect a large ball. In order to do this relatively simple task, the child has to learn about 'large', about the meaning of 'collect', about one-to-one correspondence, about taking a turn to 'collect' the 'large' ball and to negotiate the space between the actions. In this situation the learning outcomes are not related to games playing but to mathematical concepts, to spatial orientation and to social training. It is important that teachers are aware that some learning objectives can have multiple subject learning outcomes and that many learning objectives supposed to be contained within one subject specialism cannot be separated from holistic learning. Teachers also need to know about the learning potential which exists, and maximise this as far as possible. Since every curriculum-maker operates on some kind of theory of learning, it is useful in INSET activities, for example, to formulate such a theory and to discuss it in concrete terms. In this way, teachers can check whether the theory is workable and whether there are implications for the delivery of the curriculum.

EDUCATIONAL EXPERIENCES AND OBJECTIVES

In posing the question about what educational experiences can be provided to attain learning objectives, Tyler says that 'the term, "learning experience", is not the same as the content with which a course deals nor the activities of the teacher' (1949: 63). The essence of providing learning experiences is to appreciate that if the learning objectives are to be achieved then the teachers need to be knowledgeable about which learning conditions are most likely to motivate the pupils. It is important, for instance, to ensure that if a particular objective is to be achieved, the pupils should be given the correct type of learning experience. Again, in PE, an example of this would be that in order to learn the skill of catching a ball, pupils should be offered many learning experiences connected with eye–hand co-ordination, such as handling a ball in various situations, collecting a rolling ball, passing a ball to and from another and so on. If, at the same time, they are supposed to be fulfilling the objective of developing positive attitudes, then the teacher would have to build in some form of learning experience connected with sharing the ball-handling experience with another person, or becoming involved in a whole class game where the pupils have to take a turn or wait to be involved in a particular part of the game. If the enjoyment 'factor' is present as well, then so much the better! It is also important to provide experiences which are commensurate with the pupils' developmental stage. Edwards and Knight (1995: 25) state that 'Education is about working with the developing child to build worthwhile knowledge'. By knowledge, they explain, they mean not only facts, but also skills and procedures, as well as interrelated concepts.

Other factors which may arise should be considered as part of a whole school policy. These are learning experiences which might be part of a Physical Education curriculum but which have common outcomes, for example, social guidance, and learning experiences offered within Physical Education which have many outcomes in other areas, for example, understanding mathematical concepts, the acquisition of language, a knowledge and understanding of science, and knowledge about their own bodies and personal health. Permeating all learning experiences in the Physical Education curriculum should be the provision of experiences which will help all the pupils understand the purposes of their actions, and experiences which will help them think, plan and evaluate their activities.

HOW CAN LEARNING EXPERIENCES BE ORGANISED FOR EFFECTIVE INSTRUCTION?

Here, Tyler's question would seem to be the key to the successful delivery of the curriculum, and there are many recent publications which could help teachers as they consider how to develop an effective curriculum. For example, Edwards and Knight in their book *Effective Early Years Education* (1995) give a concise and accessible guide to the complex issues which face early years practitioners and offer practical solutions. Abbott and Rodger in their book *Quality Education in the Early Years* (1994) offer a collection of case studies, each one tackling a different issue. Moyles in the book *The Excellence of Play* (1995) approaches the question of how play is conceptualised, whilst Anning in *The First Years at School* (1991) offers a practical and reflective discussion based on a sympathetic recognition of the complexities of being an early years teacher. All these publications would be useful for teachers in stimulating their thinking about how the whole curriculum should be organised effectively.

However, there is not such a plethora of authors offering information about how to organise the Physical Education curriculum in the early years so that effective education can be realised. Most offer suggestions for the content of the curriculum, whilst some offer suggestions for schemes of work and units of work which curriculum co-ordinators should find helpful in the organisation of the curriculum. Perhaps it is the nature of the subject which persuades authors that because Physical Education is about activity, there is not the same need to apply theoretical frameworks to its delivery. There has certainly been a pressing desire from teachers to be given lesson-by-lesson frameworks to which Physical Education specialists have responded. A considerable number of early years teachers have said that they are already too heavily committed to teaching and assessing the core subjects in the National Curriculum to have the time to read books which do not give a 'quick fix' approach to the teaching of Physical Education lessons. It is a view with which one can sympathise. However, it is a pity that many teachers do not question why they are teaching a particular lesson, and do not consider the learning objectives which such a lesson will promote. The education in physical 'education' lectures in initial teacher training courses does not improve the situation either, mainly because the hours of lectures for the foundation subjects on initial teacher training courses has been severely reduced. Consequently, the new wave of entrants to the profession are now receiving even less information about how children learn through an involvement in Physical Education and so, in turn, will have less information to pass on to students on teaching practices when they themselves become teachers.

However, one positive factor is the continued government funding for the education of curriculum co-ordinators, who are now in a position to influence the delivery of an effective curriculum. The Physical Education co-ordinator is the key figure in planning an effective PE curriculum and ensuring that it is delivered. Since the co-ordinator is normally a full-time class teacher, the role should be carefully defined. The following list suggests the type of role and the areas of responsibility which the co-ordinator should have.
They should:

- work closely with the head teacher;
- set a good example in their own Physical Education practices;

- have a good knowledge of the Physical Education area of learning;
- attend courses to keep up to date with new developments;
- stimulate interest in the Physical Education area of learning;
- plan a Physical Education policy based on whole staff discussion;
- draw up a scheme of work after presenting a preferred selection to the staff and agreeing a consensus;
- agree with the staff which learning objectives should be achieved and which of these could be taught across the curriculum;
- draw up an agreed method of reporting the pupils' performances to parents;
- ensure that the agreed curriculum is taught;
- weekly, fortnightly or termly plans which teachers write should be collected to evaluate whether they are informed by the agreed scheme of work and the policy document;
- evaluate the success of the delivery of the agreed curriculum annually;
- manage the budget and keep records of purchases;
- collect and buy resources (books, tapes, videos, equipment, apparatus) to assist the staff to deliver the agreed curriculum;
- ensure that storage areas are easily accessible for children and staff and that stored equipment is easy to transport;
- ensure that large gymnastic equipment is readily accessible to children;
- arrange the outdoor environment so that teachers can use it effectively in lesson times and children at playtimes;
- monitor the use of the resources and ensure that resources are constantly available;
- evaluate any emergent new schemes such as Top Play and decide whether to integrate them into the agreed curriculum;
- advise other teachers when requested;
- arrange in-house INSET courses for staff;
- ensure that any cross-curricular, whole school topic webs include Physical Education;
- press for an equal share of INSET time within the foundation subjects allocation;
- discuss the provision of after-school clubs and provide staff with information about other agencies, such as local gymnastics clubs and sports centre children's clubs;
- discuss with staff when they will take their children to any sites in the locality such as parks, playgrounds and sports centres to ensure that the children are aware of activity areas which they could visit with guardians out of school time.
- discuss with the staff how physical learning objectives can be incorporated into educational day visits;
- ensure that appraisal procedures include an analysis of the co-ordinator

role and that requests for further attendance at courses is sympathet-ically reviewed.

The co-ordinator is usually given the added responsibility for overseeing the writing of the school curriculum policy. Richardson (1996: 50) suggests that a,

> good test of whether a policy is written in an accessible way, explaining how the subject should be approached and taught by all staff, is to present it to a newly qualified teacher to see whether they understand it or not. If it does not provide them with clear guidance then the policy should be re-written.

To help those teachers who may have become co-ordinators, a framework for the construction of a Physical Education policy document is offered below. A policy document should be written so that it can be easily understood by parents, governors and teachers. It should be written in simple language and should avoid specialist jargon. Richardson suggests that the more detail which is offered at this stage the less detail and time teachers should require for short-term planning.

The policy document should describe:

- what takes place in the subject and why;
- where and how often it takes place;
- how progress through the curriculum will be achieved by the children;
- how attainment will be assessed, recorded and reported to parents.

A suggested pattern of development might be to write statements about:

- the relationship of the policy to the whole school policy;
- why Physical Education is an important learning medium for pupils;
- any special circumstances which might affect the delivery of the National Curriculum;
- resources: include information on indoor and outdoor spaces and any nearby facilities which are used;
- safety: suggest clothing and footwear to be worn, removal of jewellery, wearing glasses, length of hair, expectancy in relation to personal hygiene, procedure for pupils wishing to be excluded from participa-tion, safety in practice (reference should be given for *Safe Practice in Physical Education* BAALPE 1995 and the relevant pages), method of reporting and recording accidents and procedures for first and other aid, safety as a learning process for pupils;
- aims, objectives;
- planning: the processes through which the aims and objectives will be achieved;
- timetable: when areas of work are to be blocked at different times of the year, for example, if games are only taught in the summer because of

environmental difficulties or if swimming is to be included, a statement about the reasons for this method of planning should be given;

- wet weather contingency planning: alternative active ideas for the classroom which might be science/exercise related;
- National Curriculum: the Programme of Study and the General Requirements can be included and a statement given about how the school intends to deliver them;
- reference should be made to the school Physical Education curriculum which will contain schemes of work and units of work for both groups in Key Stage 1, and details for the reception class (pre-school classes might have a separate document);
- children with special needs: guidelines should be clear about statemented children, particularly the role and responsibilities of auxiliary helpers and any other adult helpers who should be made aware of the whole school philosophy in relation to the successful integration of this group of children;
- gifted children;
- extra-curricular activities: clubs, visits, special events diary;
- assessment and reporting procedures;
- appendix, listing all resources and their location.

The organisation of the Physical Education curriculum should not be an arduous task for schools. The National Curriculum for Key Stage 1 is divided into three specific activity areas which should be given equal amounts of time. If the children are to receive a balanced curriculum, the simplest plan would be for each class to receive one lesson in each activity area each week. Some schools, however, choose to teach dance and gymnastics in the winter months and games in the summer months. The reason for using this model of planning is that there is a better chance of teaching outdoor lessons in the summer months. There is little evidence to suggest that this is a flawed planning model, other than the fact that the children have less opportunity to develop both the social and physical skills which are so important for successful play in school playgrounds and the fact that in order to acquire and develop the large and fine motor skills associated with the skills which are learned during this important life phase (Sugden 1990, Gallahue 1989), practice on a regular basis is of paramount importance. In addition, this model is not supportive of John Major's Action Agenda (Department of National Heritage 1996) which suggests that schools should focus on competitive games. Some schools have adopted a planning model which consists of a daily lesson of Physical Education which lasts for 20 minutes. In this model two lessons are devoted to gymnastics, one to games, one to dance and one to dramatic movement in the first two terms, whilst in the summer term three lessons are devoted to games and one lesson each for gymnastics and dance.

HOW CAN THESE PURPOSES BE ACHIEVED?

A legitimate response to Tyler's fourth question, formulated in 1949, would be to examine it in the light of the National Curriculum and suggest that any answer would be structured around assessment, evaluation and recording. If this is an acceptable way to proceed, then, at the outset of any discussion, it would be important to re-emphasise that there is no statutory requirement to assess pupils' performance in Physical Education. However, there is a statutory duty to report pupils' progress to parents. Dearing has said that:

> assessment is fundamental to good teaching. By making assessments during the key stage you build up your knowledge of individual pupils' strengths and limitations, which will help you in your teaching. By judging at the end of the key stage the extent to which a pupil's performance relates to the end of the key stage descriptions set out in the National Curriculum Orders, you will provide important information for pupils, their parents and your colleagues.
>
> (ACAC and SCAA 1996: i)

How should such assessment be organised? In the pre-National Curriculum era, educationists in some subjects, including Physical Education, had begun to provide tick-lists for teachers to help them to focus on skills which children should acquire naturally if the learning objectives were to be fulfilled. These became a useful tool, which teachers found helpful. The lists were drawn up by specialist Physical Educationists who were researching in the fields of physical development, acquisition of skills and the sociology and psychology of learning. Unfortunately, this type of tick-list is now thought to be superficial and not an accurate method of representing each child's abilities. The problem now is how to find an assessment tool which will on the one hand be a true and accurate representation and on the other hand be quick and easy for the teachers to use.

Simple observation is, of course, a powerful tool, and all teachers use it. It could be argued that lessons cannot be successful unless teachers observe children as they respond to the physical tasks set and accommodate the children's responses into the weekly planning of the children's learning. But the interpretation of observation is not always easy without some framework to which to refer, together with a means of recording the observations. Because teachers are already stressed from an overload of core curriculum work, what is needed is a strategy for assessment which can be used in the normal lesson time. It is important that critical learning objectives should be integrated into the activities contained within the three activity areas in some sort of order. This would have the effect of sharpening the teachers' observation of the children without having to interrupt normal lesson procedures. The assessment items, therefore, should be part of the normal Programme of Study. One way to achieve this would be to set up a curriculum model, using the information in the earlier chapters of this book as guidance. The content in these chapters presents a developmental curriculum based on the research evidence which is available to inform practitioners of the learning objectives which children in this life phase should be able to acquire. If the material is taught in sequential order, then at the end of each week, teachers will be able to evaluate each of the three areas of activity and locate any children who might be having problems. Teachers can then make their own decisions about whether to repeat lessons or group the children in different ways so that they can have more direct impact on the children's learning.

Another method of proceeding would be for schools to decide what the critical learning objectives are and to choose the 'test items' which would be the focus of a Physical Education curriculum. Bate and Smith, for example, formulated a manual for nursery assessment in 1978 which included test items concerned with manual and tool skills (thirty-eight items) and physical skills (forty-one items) which could have been used for a very successful framework for a Physical Education programme for younger children. If teachers wanted to set up such a model they could choose practical test items based on the three areas of activity in the Programme of Study and these could be the foundation of the Physical Education curriculum. By using such a model, teachers would be constantly assessing the children's performance in relation to the required objectives and they would not have to make special arrangements.

By the end of Key Stage 1, pupils should have achieved the following targets, as listed in the End of Key Stage Description:

> Pupils plan and perform simple skills safely, and show control in linking actions together. They improve their performance through practising their skills, working alone and with a partner. They talk about what they and others have done, and are able to make simple judgements. They recognise and describe changes that happen to their bodies during exercise.

> These descriptions describe the type and range of performance that the majority of pupils should characteristically demonstrate by the end of the key stage, having been taught the relevant programme of study.
> (Department for Education and Employment 1995: 11)

Linked to the whole question of assessment is the necessity of recording the information. There is no doubt that the pupil records which have been compiled by the teacher who taught the child in the previous year are of inestimable value, but this is particularly true when the child is about to enter the last year and phase of Key Stage 1. End of Year 1 reports can be of use to both the child and the parents, in that they tell what progress is being made and indicate to the teacher the stage which the child has reached. Additionally, teachers then have an opportunity to plan a programme which might, first, revisit some of the Year 1 curriculum and, second, adopt teaching methods which will give the teacher more opportunities to arrange one-on-one directed teaching. A typical report for a pupil entering Year 2 is outlined below. It gives the type of information needed to create a report/assessment based on the SCAA recommendations, evaluates it, and suggests a further plan of action.

Lisa (age 6, entering Year 2)

Games

Lisa plays actively during whole class games with the teacher, but finds difficulty in sustaining concentration when asked to practise with a partner or a small group. She has acquired the fundamental skills of running and skipping, but has difficulty in hopping for sustained periods. She does not enjoy chasing games. She has some difficulty in manual dexterity skills concerned with catching, throwing and bouncing a ball and whilst she can kick a stationary ball, she cannot dribble the ball with her feet.

Gymnastic activities

Lisa has acquired the skills of travelling on her hands and feet, can turn when walking but has difficulty in turning when running and jumping. She has difficulty in balancing, particularly when asked to walk along a bench. She rolls competently using a pencil roll but has not yet acquired either a forward or backward roll. Lisa is not able to swing on a rope. She is starting to climb to low heights with more confidence, although she is still timid about jumping from apparatus. She can link a series of actions together on the floor but is not yet competent on apparatus.

Dance

Lisa enjoys dancing to music and performs all limb movements well when she works from a static base. She dances freely to music but finds jumping, turning and balancing difficult. She can perform and repeat patterns which she has created. She has a 'keen ear' for music and expresses herself well. She has a good response to rhythmic pieces.

Lisa is competent at offering comments about her own and other pupils' performances and is showing a growing ability to make simple judgements. Lisa is able to recognise the changes which happen to her body when she is taking part in exercise and can describe such changes in an articulate manner.

Teacher evaluation and action plan

- Lisa can best be described as not yet achieving the attainment target. She needs one-to-one help in developing both her manual dexterity skills and her bodily balance.
- Her posture is suspect. She seems to be developing a curvature of the spine. She is not always as active as she might be.
- Check her manual dexterity in other skills (keyboard, writing) and her eye–hand co-ordination.
- Check her oral skills record which appears to be good, check her attainment in music which would appear to be above average at this time.
- Plan groupwork to enable more directed teaching opportunities. Check the balancing problem: is it a physical problem? Or is she timid?

The End of Key Stage Report can have the same format as the Year 1 report but there may be central issues which will affect the planning of the first year Programme of Study for Key Stage 2. Part of the report may be concerned with the fact that the pupils have not received any swimming lessons, or that inclement weather for three months prevented the full delivery of the Programme of Study in the games area of activity. Two case studies are offered below.

Stephen (age 7, end of Key Stage 1)

Games

Stephen always works with enthusiasm and energy. He concentrates on all practices whether working alone, with a partner or when playing in a group. He is competent at throwing overarm and bowling underarm and is accurate when directing balls with his hands. He can catch large and small balls when thrown by another player. He is competent at travelling with a ball using his feet and in passing the ball with accuracy. He likes chasing, dodging, and defending his space, particularly when playing goalie.

Gymnastic activities

Stephen is competent at performing the basic actions of travelling using his hands and feet, turning, rolling, jumping, balancing, swinging and climbing, both on the floor and on apparatus. He can link a series of actions together both when on the floor and when on apparatus and can repeat them. He can plan his own sequence of movements and is always ready to refine his movements if shown how. He concentrates on practising any movements which are suggested.

Dance

Stephen responds readily to instructions, but he finds exploring moods and feelings through dance actions somewhat bemusing. He is competent when actively engaged in rhythmic traditional dances where a framework is provided, but does not show the same competency when in a creative framework. He shows competence when given teacher-directed movements to perform.

Stephen is able to plan sequences, but is seldom willing to comment on other pupils' work unless specifically asked. He does not seem interested in the changes which occur in his body when he is involved in exercise and whilst he recognises the short-term effects of exercise, he would rather be active than talking. He is beginning to play fairly, although he is not always tolerant of those less capable than himself. He has good posture in all situations.

Teacher evaluation and action plan

• Stephen displays some of the End of Key Stage Descriptions for Key Stage 2 pupils in two activity areas but does not demonstrate the full range of attributes for successful completion of the Programme of Study for dance.
• Check his writing, art and music attainments. Does his profile indicate a lack of creativity? Is his work more objective and scientific? Or is he an 'action man'?
• Should I alter my teaching style and make it less open-ended in dance lessons? Should I group the children according to ability in games lessons?
• Stephen should be encouraged to join a gymnastics club and should be encouraged to become a member of the school football squad.

Hadad (age 7, end of Key Stage 1)

Teachers might want to exclude the information in brackets when writing a report for parents.

Games

(Hadad is very verbal when she considers, 'it's not fair !') She is not able yet to cope with limitations in her own performance. Her own performance of the basic skills is limited (because she is overweight). She can run, skip and hop but has difficulty in sustaining her practices for any length of time. She can catch a ball thrown by the teacher, but can not throw straight. She can kick a ball but without accuracy. She has difficulty in dribbling a ball with her feet and bouncing a ball with her hands.

Gymnastic activities

Hadad responds well to instructions (but finds difficulty in managing her body weight). Travelling on hands and feet is difficult. She can run and skip but has difficulty in jumping, particularly from apparatus. She finds difficulty in balancing (her weight) in all situations. She can plan a sequence of movements both on the floor and on apparatus at her own ability level and she can repeat the movements.

Dance

Hadad is responsive to moods generated by various musical pieces and percussion instruments. She can create simple rhythms on percussion instruments for others to dance to. She can plan, perform and talk about dances which she creates. She is unable to control her body in the air whilst running, jumping or skipping, but her use of gesture from a static base is outstanding. She is also able to show an understanding of the use of various levels and speeds in creating texture and shape in various patterns when performing from a static base.

Hadad is able to plan, perform and evaluate her movements and can comment with accuracy on other pupils' performances. She has good posture when walking. (She is not as active as she should be. She is not able to come to terms with the limitations in her own performance and wastes time gaining the teacher's attention.) She responds readily to instructions in dance.
She articulates well and can explain why performers should warm up for and recover from exercise.

Teacher evaluation and action plan

- Hadad is not yet able to fulfil all the requirements listed for the three activity areas in the Programme of Study.
- Hadad meets all the End of Key Stage Descriptions except in her lack of ability to 'show control in linking actions together'.

- Is she prevented from reaching satisfactory achievement of the attainment target because of her body weight?
- Check that she is not underachieving in any other subject area. Is she able to sustain work in other areas without showing signs of fatigue?
- Check her file. Is the overweight condition the result of a genetic or family problem? Has she a motor deficiency problem?
- Use the classroom health project to focus sensitively on the need to balance food intake with energy expenditure.
- Build up Hadad's self-worth in dance lessons where she is showing outstanding ability.
- Start an extra-curricular dance club.

Clearly these observations would be taking place throughout the year and teachers, as always, would be recording this data mentally. In all cases the teachers would not wait until the end of the year before acting on the pupil data listed above. They would want to act on the observations as the various needs of the pupils became evident. In Hadad's case this is crucially important if the problem is causing multi-curricular difficulties for her. Equally, Lisa has two physical 'problem' areas which will need immediate attention if she is to reach her potential in all activity areas. A lack of ability to balance is an indicator of several medical conditions, some concerned with ear infections, some with sensory conditions and some with motor deficiency problems, all of which should be given urgent attention. Stephen, however, whilst showing evidence of outstanding levels of performance in all three activity areas, is the most likely candidate in these three case studies to be neglected in relation to receiving the type of teaching which he needs. Children who show giftedness in Physical Education in the early years are often celebrated but seldom helped to achieve their potential.

In order to record observations of pupils' performance attainments, some schools have adopted a process which allows teachers to record pupil information relevant to the End of Key Stage Descriptions, and the objectives listed for the three activity areas as and when it arises. This saves valuable teacher time at the reporting date at the end of the year. In these schools teachers are encouraged to write down anything which they think might be appropriate in building up a pupil profile at any time. In addition the information can be reviewed at the end of each week, when planning is taking place for the following week's lessons. There is no doubt that despite the outcry when the recording of pupil's progress was first proposed, this type of observation has enabled teachers to find out more about their pupils. It has also fine-tuned the observation skills of early years teachers.

The last, but equally important evaluation procedure which should be examined when consideration is given to whether the policy and the agreed curriculum are resulting in acceptable pupil achievement and progression, is the evaluation of the curriculum and its delivery. It would be less than realistic to suggest that this procedure should be carried out by a whole staff evaluation each year, but it is a task which the co-ordinator should engage in annually. Once the evaluation is complete the co-ordinator can then consider whether there is a need to engage the head teacher in any discussions in relation to the evaluation and to decide together whether INSET action is needed.

Evaluation can begin with writing a list of perceived positive and negative points based on both a review of the pupils' records together with assessments noted throughout the year. A list of positive points could include:

- the staff in the Junior department seem pleased with the standard of our children's performance when they enter KS2 and found our record sheet helpful;
- all staff have used their designated PE timetabled times;
- the reception class teachers had a meeting with the nursery class teachers;
- The Year 2 teachers have produced good records after my input on selecting indicators of performance;
- The staff seem to have learned a great deal from the in-house INSET afternoon on how to achieve progression in gymnastics;
- I was able to balance the budget;
- The new schemes of work seem to be helping the children to make progress;
- Employing an auxiliary for the children with special needs seems to be successful;
- The style sheet for recording the children's progress is giving valuable assessment evidence;
- The staff are using the gymnastics video which we agreed to buy;
- The new gymnastics club is helping the children to improve their performance and it is increasing the self-worth of all the children involved.

A list of negative points might include:

- Miss B is not taking her outdoor games lessons;
- the student on teaching practice did not seem clear about our policy document;
- why are the staff not asking for any advice?
- I have not seen anybody using the new dance cassettes which we agreed to buy;
- it is taking too long for the children to erect the large apparatus. Could we store it so that it is more accessible?

- I need more money to build up the stock of games equipment;
- the recording and reporting style sheet is not successful;
- parents are unhappy about the lack of extra-curricular sport clubs;
- the school playing field is becoming a thoroughfare for local shoppers;
- the governors are unhappy because we have agreed to cancel a competitive sports day.

The co-ordinator should then draw up an action agenda, listing the actions needed in priority order. For example, some of the points listed are concerns which must be discussed with the head teacher, some are issues which should be shared with the whole staff and some with other curriculum co-ordinators, whilst some are issues which require personal self-evaluation.

The challenge for the co-ordinator would seem to produce a heavy workload for a class teacher. However, many co-ordinators will have already followed a main course in Physical Education whilst in training, and will have also taken part in an INSET co-ordinators' course, both experiences giving them a head start in managing various action agendas and dealing with any problems which arise. It should also be remembered, too, that the role of curriculum co-ordinator gives class teachers valuable experience which could lead to them gaining senior positions in primary schools.

Resources

PRE-SCHOOL

Dance ideas

Kate Harrison (1992) *Look! Look What I Can Do!* 2nd edn, London: BBC Publications (80 Wood Lane, London, W12 OTT)

Primrose Educational Publishing
White Cross
Lancaster   LA1 4XQ

EDRA Physical Education system and activity play

ASCO Educational Supplies Ltd.
19 Lockwood Way
Parkside Lane
Leeds   LS11 5TH

Games equipment

Davies the Sports People
Ludlow Hill Road
West Bridgford
Nottingham   NG2 6HD

Games schemes

Teddy PEGS and PEGS (Physical Education Games Scheme)
Physical Education Association of the United Kingdom
Suite 5
10 Churchill Square
Kings Hill
West Malling
Kent   ME19 4DU

Gymnastic equipment

Davies the Sports People
Ludlow Hill Road
West Bridgford
Nottingham   NG2 6HD

Carr Early Years Range
Ronald Street
Radford
Nottingham
NG7 3GY

Universal Services
Beckingham Business Park
Tolleshunt Major
Maldon
Essex   CM8 LZ

Gymnastic activities clubs

Gym Babes and Tumble Tots
Blue Bird Park
Bromsgrove Road
Hunnington
Halesowen
West Midlands   B62 OTT

Gymnastic video

Gymnastic and Movement Skills for Pre-school and Nursery Levels
Sutcliffe Leisure Ltd.
Sutcliffe Sport
Lynn Lane
Shenstone
Lichfield
Staffs   WS14 OEE

Music for Dance

The Carnival of Animals (C. Saint-Saëns, 1886)
Cats (Andrew Lloyd Webber, 1986)
Children's Classics (P. Dukas, P. Prokofiev and C. Saint-Saëns, 1996)
'Coming round again' (Carly Simon, on *Greatest Hits Live*, 1988, Arista)
Disney Hits (various artists, 1986)

'Enya/Watermark' (Enya and N. Ryan, 1988)
Favourite Sports Themes (Powerpack Orchestra, 1988)
Going to the Zoo (Early Learning Centre Collection, 1995)
'The grasshopper's dance' (Bucalossi/J. Hylton, on *Hello Children Every-where*, 1988, EMI)
'Morning' from *Peer Gynt Suite* (E. Grieg, 1888)
The Nutcracker (P.I. Tchaikovsky, 1892)
'Radetzsky-Marsch' (J. Strauss the elder, 1848)
'The Stars and Stripes forever' (J.P. Sousa, 1897)

Outdoor equipment and apparatus

Community Playthings
Robertsbridge
East Sussex   TN32 5DR

Record Playground Equipment
Waterford Complex
Selby
North Yorkshire   Y08 8AP

Russell Leisure Products
Box 415
Roddinglaw Road
Gogar
Edinburgh   EH12 9GW

SMP Playgrounds
Pound Road
Chertsey
Surrey   KT16 8EJ

Wicksteed Leisure
Digby Street
Kettering
Northamptonshire   NN16 8YJ

Soft play

Wesco UK
Wesco House
3 Brown's Lane
Coventry
Warwickshire   CV5 9DT

Universal Services
Beckingham Business Park
Tolleshunt Major
Maldon
Essex   CM8 LZ

GYMNASTIC ACTIVITIES: KEY STAGE 1

Large apparatus

Continental Sports Ltd
Paddock
Huddersfield
West Yorkshire   HD1 4SD

Carr Gymnastic Equipment
Ronald Street
Radford
Nottingham   NG7 3GY

Davies the Sports People
Ludlow Hill Road
West Bridgford
Nottingham   NG2 6HD

Evans of Longton Ltd.
Mercury House
Sutherland Road
Stoke-on-Trent   STD 1JD

Universal Services
Beckingham Business Park
Tolleshunt Major
Maldon
Essex   CM8 LZ

GAMES: KEY STAGE 1

Equipment

Davies the Sports People
Ludlow Hill Road
West Bridgford
Nottingham   NG2 6HD

(SPORDAS Range, magic spots, coloured balls, bats and an extensive range of other games apparatus.)

Wesco UK
Wesco House
3 Brown's Lane
Allesley
Coventry   CV5 9DT
(Storage chests, space markers, cones, motor education bags, balls and equipment trolleys.)

Games schemes

PEGS (with badge awards)
Physical Education Association of the United Kingdom
Suite 5
10 Churchill Square
Kings Hill
West Malling
Kent   ME19 4DU

Top Play
The Youth Sports Trust
9 Whitehall
London   SW1A 2DD

DANCE

BBC Broadcasts
Let's Move (4–5-year-olds) and *Time to Move* (6–8-year-olds)
20-minute programmes, Radio 3, weekly in term-time

BBC Education Information
White City
201 Wood Lane
London   W12 7TS
(Supplies five cassettes to be used with ten lesson notes to create a programme of folk dancing.)

English Folk Dance and Song Society
Cecil Sharpe House
London   NW1 7AY
(Provides periodicals, courses/conferences, information, books and music.)

Percussion Plus
Ludlow Hill Road
West Bridgford
Nottingham   NG2 6HD
(Supplies a wide variety of instruments.)

MUSIC

Most of the recorded music listed below can be obtained from local music shops.
'Appalachian spring' (A. Copland, 1944)
Bolero (Le Tombeau de Couperin) (M. Ravel, 1928)
The Carnival of Animals (C. Saint-Saëns, 1886)
Cats (Andrew Lloyd Webber, 1986)
Children's Classics (P. Dukas, P. Prokofiev and C. Saint-Saëns, 1996)
'Circus polka' (I. Stravinsky, 1942)
'Clown's dance' from *Circus* (J. Ibert, 1952, from the film *Invitation to the Dance*, 1954)
'Coming round again' (Carly Simon, on *Greatest Hits Live*, 1988, Arista)
'Dance of the tumblers' from *The Snow Maiden* (N.A. Rimsky-Korsakov, 1881)
'Danse macabre' (C. Saint-Saëns, 1874)
Disney Hits (various artists, 1986)
The Draughtsman's Contract (Michael Nyman, 1983)
'Enya/Watermark' (Enya and N. Ryan, 1988)
'Fantasia on Greensleeves' (R. Vaughan Williams, on *The Classic Experience*, 1988, EMI)
Favourite Sports Themes (Powerpack Orchestra, 1988)
Four Seasons (A. Vivaldi, 1725)
Going to the Zoo (Early Learning Centre Collection, 1995)
'The grasshopper's dance' (Bucalossi/J. Hylton, on *Hello Children Everywhere*, 1988, EMI)
La Mer (Après-midi d'un faune) (C. Debussy, 1903–5)
'Morning' from *Peer Gynt Suite* (E. Grieg, 1888)
The Nutcracker (P.I. Tchaikovsky, 1892)
'Overture' from *Candide* (L. Bernstein, 1956)
Pastoral Symphony (L.V. Beethoven, 1807)
'Radetzky-Marsch' (J. Strauss the elder, 1848)
'The return of the gladiators' (Storm, 1993)
Sacred Spirit: Chants and Dances of the Native Indians (1996, Virgin)
'The Stars and Stripes forever' (J.P. Sousa, 1897)

'Summertime' (G. and I. Gershwin, on *The George Gershwin Collection*, various artists, 1987, Deja Vu)

'Swing low sweet chariot' from *Spirituals* (sung by H.E. Porter and his gospel singers)

'Take five' (P. Desmond and I. Brubeck, on *The Collection – Dave Brubeck*, 1985 Deja vu)

'You make me feel (mighty real)' (Sylvester, 1989, Southbound)

USEFUL ADDRESSES

Arts Council of Great Britain
Dance Department
14 Peter Street
London   SWI 3NQ
(Provides information.)

Amateur Swimming Association
Harold Fern House
Derby Square
Loughborough
Leicestershire   LE11 OAL
(Swimming schemes and swimming awards, provides courses/conferences and supplies books, periodicals and information.)

British Association of Early Childhood Education
111 City View House
463 Bethnal Green Road
London   E2 9QY
(Provides courses/conferences and supplies information.)

British Amateur Gymnastics Association
Ford Hall
Lilleshall National Sports Centre
Newport
Shropshire   TF10 9MB
(Schemes and awards, provides courses/conferences and information, and supplies books.)

British Sports Association for the Disabled
Solecast House
13–27 Brunswick Place
London   N1 6DX
(Provides information.)

The Dyspraxia Trust
PO Box 30
Hitchin
Herts   SG5 1UU
(Provides information and supplies booklets.)

The English Sports Council
16 Upper Woburn Place
London   WC1H OQP
(Provides information and addresses of Regional Sports Councils and National Governing Bodies of Sport in England.)

The Health Education Authority
Hamilton House
Mabledon Place
London   WC1H 9TX
(Provides information.)

PROFESSIONAL MAGAZINE

Primary PE Focus
The Physical Education Association of the United Kingdom
Suite 5
10 Churchill Square
Kings Hill
West Malling
Kent   ME19 4DU

Bibliography

Abbot, L. and Rodger, R. (1994) *Quality Education in the Early Years*, Milton Keynes: Open University Press.

ACAC and SCAA (1996) *A Guide to the National Curriculum in Physical Education*, London: HMSO.

Alderson, J. and Crutchley, D. (1990) 'Physical education and the National Curriculum', in *New Directions in Physical Education*, vol. 1, Leeds: Human Kinetics.

Anderson, N.H. and Cuneo, D.O. (1978) 'The height and width rule in children's judgements of quality', *Journal of Experimental Psychology,* 107: 335–78.

Anning, A. (1991) *The First Years at School*, Milton Keynes: Open University Press.

Armstrong, N. (1990) 'Children's activity patterns: the implications for Physical Education' in *New Directions in Physical Education*, vol. 1, Champaign, Illinois: Human Kinetics.

Armstrong, N. and Biddle, S. (1992) 'Health related physical activity in the National Curriculum', in *New Directions in Physical Education*, vol. 2, Champaign, Illinois: Human Kinetics.

Armstrong, N. and McManus, A. (1996) 'Growth maturation and Physical Education', in *New Directions in Physical Education*, vol. 3, London: Cassells.

Arts Council of Great Britain (1993) *Dance in Schools*, London: Arts Council.

Athey, C. (1990) *Extending Thought in Young Children: A Parent–Teacher Partnership*, London: Paul Hamlyn.

Aubrey, C. (ed.) (1994) *The Role of Subject Knowledge in the Early Years of Schooling*, London: Falmer Press.

BAALPE (1995) *Safe Practice in Physical Education*, Saltwell: Saltwell Education Centre.

Baranowski, T., Thompson, W.O., Du Rant, R.H., Baranowski, J. and Phul, J. (1993) 'Observations on physical activity in physical locations: age, gender, ethnicity, and month effects', *Research Quarterly on Exercise and Sport*, 64(2): 127–33.

Bate, M. and Smith, M. (1978) *Manual for Assessment in Nursery Education*, Windsor: NFER-Nelson.

Bate, M., Smith, M. and James, J. (1982) *Review of Tests and Assessments in Early Education (3–5 Years)*, Windsor: NFER-Nelson.

Bee, H. (1995) *The Growing Child*, New York: Harper-Collins.

Benn, T. and Benn, B. (1995) *Primary Gymnastics: A Multi-activities Approach*, Cambridge: Cambridge University Press.

Berry, P. (1993) 'Young children's use of fixed playground equipment', *International Play Journal*, 1(2).

Blenkin, G. and Kelly, A.V. (1987) *Early Childhood: A Developmental Curriculum*, London: Paul Chapman.

Blenkin, G. and Yue, N. (1994) 'Profiling early years practitioners: some impressions from a national survey', *Early Years*, 15(1): 13–22.

Blenkin, G. and Yue, N. (1995) *Principles into Practice: The Quality of Children's Early Learning*, on-going research project, London: Goldsmith's College, University of London.

Bower, T.G.R. (1966) 'The development of motor behaviour – walking', in M.Roberts and J. Tamburrini (eds) *Child Development 0–5*, Edinburgh: Holmes McDougall.

Bradley, L. (1989) 'Predicting learning difficulties', in J.J. Dumont and H. Nakken (eds) *Learning Disabilities: Cognitive, Social and Remedial Aspects*, Amsterdam: Swets Publishing.

Brown, A. (1987) *Active Games for Children with Movement Difficulties*, London: Harper & Row.

Bruce, V. (1988) *Movement and Dance in the Primary School*, Milton Keynes: Open University Press.

Bruner, J. (1980) *Under Five in Britain*, London: Grant McIntyre.

Buckham, J. (1994) 'Teachers' understanding of children's drawing', in C. Aubrey (ed.) *The Role of Subject Knowledge in the Early Years of Schooling*, London: Falmer Press.

Buhler, C. (1935) *From Birth to Maturity*, London: Routledge.

Bunker, D., Hardy, C., Smith, B. and Almond, L. (1994) *Primary Physical Education: Implementing the National Curriculum*, Cambridge: Cambridge University Press.

Chartered Society of Physiotherapists (1995) Press release, London.

Chedzoy, S. (1996) *Physical Education for Teachers and Coordinators at Key Stages 1 and 2*, London: David Fulton Publishers.

Cleave, S. and Sharpe, C. (1986) *The Arts: A Preparation to Teach: A Study of Initial Training for Primary Teachers*, Windsor: NFER-Nelson.

Collins, M. (1990) 'European perspectives on sport: sport as an economic and political force', *Leisure Manager*, 8(8): 40–1.

Cooper, A. (1995) *Starting Games Skills*, London: Stanley Thornes.

Cooper, M.G. (1972) *Observational Studies in Nursery School*, PhD thesis, University of Durham.

Corbin, C.B. (1973) *A Text Book of Motor Development*, Dubuque, Iowa: W.C. Brown.

Corbin, C.B. (1989) *Educational Perspective on Self-esteem: Putting it All Together for Kids*, Boston, Mass.: American Alliance for Health, Recreation and Dance.

Cratty, B.J. (1973) *Movement Behavior and Motor Learning*, New York: Meredith Publishing Company.

Curtis, A.M. (1986) *A Curriculum for the Pre-school Child: Learning to Learn*, Windsor: NFER-Nelson.

Davie, R., Butler, N. and Goldstein, H. (1972) *From Birth to Seven*, London: Longman.

Davies, A. and Sabin, V. (1995) *Bodywork*, Cheltenham: Stanley Thornes.

Davies, M. (1995) *Helping Children to Learn Through a Movement Perspective*, London: Hodder & Stoughton.

De Boo, M. (1992) *Action Rhymes and Games*, Leamington Spa: Scholastic Ltd.

Dennis, W.W. and Dennis, M. (1940) 'The effect of early cradling practices upon the onset of walking in Hopi children', *Journal of Genetic Psychology*, 56: 77–86.

Department for Education (1994) *Code of Practice on Identification and Assessment of Special Educational Needs*, London: HMSO.

Department for Education and Employment (1995) *Physical Education in the National Curriculum*, London: HMSO.

Department for Education and Employment (1996) *The Next Steps*, Nursery Education Scheme, London: HMSO.

Department of Education and Science (1978) *Curriculum 11–16*, London: HMSO.

Department of Education and Science (1990) *Starting with Quality: Report of the Committee of Enquiry into the Educational Experiences offered to Three and Four year olds* (Rumbold Report) pares 67–8, London: HMSO.

Department of Education and Science (1991) *Physical Education for Ages 5 to 16*, York: National Curriculum Council.

Department of Education and Science/Welsh Office (1991) *National Curriculum Physical Education Working Group Interim Report*, London: HMSO.

Department of Health and Social Security (1985) *National Child Development Study*, London: HMSO.

Department of Health and Social Security (1995a) *The Health of the Nation: A Report from the Nutrition and Physical Activity Task Force*, London.

Department of Health and Social Security (1995b) *National Study of Health and Growth*, London: HMSO.

Department of National Heritage (1995) *Sport: Raising the Game*, London: HMSO.

Department of National Heritage (1996) *Sport: Raising the Game: The First Year Report*, London: HMSO.

Donaldson, M. (1978) *Children's Minds*, Glasgow: Fontana/Collins.

Dowling, M. (1995) *Starting School at Four: A Joint Endeavour*, London: Paul Chapman.

Dunn, A. (1996) *Enjoy Yourself!* Durham: University of Durham.

Dyspraxia Trust (1991) *Praxis Makes Perfect*, Hitchen, Herts: Dyspraxia Trust.

Edwards, A. and Knight, P. (1995) *Effective Early Years Education*, Milton Keynes: Open University Press.

Espenschade, A.S. and Eckert, H.M. (1967) *Motor Development*, Columbus, Ohio: C. Merrill.

Exiner, J. and Lloyd, P. (1987) *Learning Through Dance*, Australia: Oxford University Press.

Fitts, P.M. and Posner, J.I. (1967) *Human Performance*, Monterey: Brookes/Cole.

Fox, K.R. (1992) 'Physical education and the development of self-esteem in children', in N. Armstrong (ed.) *New Directions in Physical Education*, vol. 2, Leeds: Human Kinetics.

Fox, K.R. (1994) 'Understanding young children and their decisions about physical activity', *British Journal of Physical Education*, 25(1): 5–19.

Fox, K.R. (1996) 'Physical activity promotion and the active school', in N. Armstrong (ed.) *New Directions in Physical Education*, vol. 3

Fraser, D.L. (1991) *Playdancing*, Pennington, NJ: Princeton Publishers.

Gabbard, L. (1991) *A Postmodern Instructor's Manual for Joel Spring's American Education*, 5th edn, London: Longmans.

Gallahue, D.L. (1989) *Motor Development*, Indianapolis: Benchmark Press Ltd.

Gallahue, D.L. (1995) *Understanding Motor Development*, 3rd edn, Wisconsin: Brown & Benchmark.

Gesell, A. (1928) *Infancy and Human Growth*, New York: Macmillan.

Gesell, A. (1940) *The First Years of Life*, New York: Harper & Row.

Gordon, N. and McKinlay, I. (1980) *Helping Clumsy Children*, Edinburgh: Churchill & Livingstone.

Graham, D. G., with Tytier, G. (1993) *A Lesson for Us All: The Making of the National Curriculum*, London: Routledge.

Graham, J. and Jeffs, H. (1993) *Art: Teaching within the National Curriculum*, Leamington Spa: Scholastic Ltd.

Gray, J. and Buttriss, J. (1993) *Trends in Patterns of Disease and Diet*, London: National Dairy Council.

Gregory, J.R., Collins, D.L., Davies, P. S. W., Hughes, J.M. and Clarke, P.C. (1995) *National Diet and Nutritional Survey: Children Aged 1.5 to 4.5 Years*, London: Department of Health.

Groves, L. (1975) *Physical Education for Slow Learning Girls in the North East of England*, MEd thesis, University of Durham.

Groves, L. (ed.) (1979) *Physical Education for Special Needs*, Cambridge, Cambridge University Press.

Groves, L. (1989) 'Children with special needs', in A. Williams (ed.) *Issues in Physical Education for the Primary Years*, London: Falmer Press.

Gulbenkian Foundation (Calouste) (1990) *Dance Education and Training in Britain*, London: Gulbenkian Foundation (Calouste).

Harlen, W. (1985) *Primary Science: Taking the Plunge*, London: Heinemann-Butterworth.

Harlow, M. and Rolfe, L. (1992) *Let's Dance: A Handbook for Teachers*, London: BBC Educational Publications.

Harrison, K. (1992) *Look! Look What I Can Do!* 2nd edn, London: BBC Educational Publications.

Harrison, K. (1993) *Let's Dance: The Place of Dance in the Primary School*, London: Hodder & Stoughton.

Harter, S. (1985) *Manual for the Self-perception Profile for Children*, Denver: University of Denver Press.

Harter, S. (1986) 'Processes underlying the construction, maintenance and enhancement of the self-concept of children', in J. Suls and A.G. Greenwald (eds) *Physiological Perspectives on the Self*, vol. 3, Hillsdale, NJ: Erlbaum, pp. 133–81.

Haywood, K. (1993) *Life Span Motor Development*, Champaign, Illinois: Human Kinetics.

Heath, W., Gregory, C., Money, J., Peat, G., Smith, J. and Stratton, G. (1994) *Physical Education Key Stage 1*, National Curriculum Blueprints series, Teachers' Resource Book, Cheltenham: Stanley Thornes.

Home Office (1995) Home Office statistics, *Observer*, November, from 'Social focus on children', Home Office Statistical Bulletins, London. From B. Botting (ed.) (1995) *The Health of our Children: Dicennial Supplement*, London: Office of Population Censuses and Statistics.

Hurst, V. (1991) *Planning for Early Learning: The Education of Under Fives*, London: Paul Chapman.

Hutt, C. (1971) 'Exploration and play in children', in R.E. Herron and B. Sutton-Smith (eds) *Child's Play*, Chichester: Wiley.

Hutt, C. (1972) *Males and Females*, Harmondsworth: Penguin.

Illingworth, R.S. (1967) *The Development of the Infant and Young Child: Normal and Abnormal*, 3rd edn, London: Livingstone.

Isaacs, S. (1938) *The Nursery Years*, London: Routledge & Kegan Paul.

Jones, C. (1996) 'Physical education at Key Stage 1' in N. Armstrong (ed.) *New Directions in Physical Education*, vol. 3, London: Cassell.

Jowsey, S.E. (1988) *Can I Play Too?* London: David Fulton Publishers.

Klesges, R.C., Eck, L.H., Hanson, C.L., Haddock, C.K. and Klesges, L.M. (1990) 'Effects of obesity, social interactions and physical environment on physical activity in preschoolers', *Health Psychology*, 9: 435–49.

Leese, S. and Packer, M. (1980) *Dance in Schools*, Oxford: Heinemann Educational Books Ltd.

Lipscomb, B. (1996) *A Policy Guide for Physical Education in the Nursery School and Reception Class*, Lancaster: Primrose Publishing.

McGraw, M.B. (1945) *The Neuromuscular Maturation of the Human Infant*, New York: Hafner.

McKinlay, I., 'Foreword' in Russell, J.P. (ed.) (1988) *Graded Activities for Children with Motor Difficulties*, Cambridge: Cambridge University Press.

McMillan, N. (1919) *The Nursery School*, London: Dent.

Malina, R.M. and Bouchard, C. (1991) *Growth, Maturation and Physical Activity*, Champaign, Illinois: Human Kinetics.

Manners, H.K. and Carroll, M.E. (1991) *Gymnastics 4–7: A Session by Session Approach*, London: Falmer Press.

Manning, K. and Sharp, A. (1977) *Structuring Play in the Early Years at School*, London: Ward Locke.

Marino, G.M. and Fiese, B.H. (1993) 'Comparison of free play mother–toddler interaction patterns in employed and at-home mothers', *International Play Journal*, 1(2): 105–14.

Matterson, E.M. (1969) *This Little Puffin: Finger Plays and Nursery Games*, Harmondsworth: Penguin.

Millar, S. (1971) *The Psychology of Play*, 3rd edn, Harmondsworth: Penguin.

Morris, L.R. and Schultz, L. (1989) *Creative Play Activities for Children with Disabilities*, Champaign, Illinois: Human Kinetics.

Moyles, J.R. (1989) *Just Playing? The Role and Status of Play in Early Childhood*, Milton Keynes: Open University Press.

Moyles, J.R. (ed.) (1995) *The Excellence of Play*, Milton Keynes: Open University Press.

OFSTED (1993) *First Class: The Standards and Quality of Education in Reception Classes*, London: HMSO.

Osborn, A.F. (1981) 'Under fives in school in England and Wales', *Educational Research*, 23(2): 96–103.

Osborn, A.F., Butler, N.R. and Morris, A.C. (1984) *The Social Life of Britain's Five Year Olds: A Report of the Child Health and Education Study*, London and Boston: Routledge & Kegan Paul.

Payne, H. (1992) *Dance Movement Therapy*, London: Routledge.

Pepitone, E.A. (1980) *Children in Cooperation and Competition*, Lexington, Mass.: Lexington Books.

Physical Education Association of the United Kingdom (PEAUK) (1987) *Physical Education in Schools*, West Malling, Kent: PEAUK.

Physical Education Association of the United Kingdom (PEAUK) (1994) *Primary PE Focus*, West Malling, Kent: (PEAUK).

Piaget, J., Inhelder, B. and Szeminska, A. (1960) *The Child's Conception of Geometry*, London: Routledge & Kegan Paul.

Preston, V. (1969) *A Handbook for Modern Educational Dance*, London: MacDonald & Evans Ltd.

Read, B. and Edwards, P. (1992) *Teaching Children to Play Games*, London: Sports Council.

Richardson, R. (1996) 'The curriculum co-ordinator', *Child Educator*, 73(9): 50–3.

Russell, J. (1965) *Creative Dance in the Primary School*, London: MacDonald Evans.

Russell, J.P. (1988) *Graded Activities for Children with Motor Difficulties*, Cambridge: Cambridge University Press.

Sarlett, W.G. (1983) 'Social isolation from age-mates among nursery school children', in M. Donaldson (ed.) *Early Childhood and Development*, Oxford: Basil Blackwell.

SCAA (1996) *Nursery Education: Desirable Outcomes for Children's Learning on Entering Compulsory Education*, London: HMSO.

SCAA and ACAC (1996a) *A Guide to the National Curriculum*, London: HMSO.

SCAA and ACAC (1996b) *Consistency in Teacher Assessment: Exemplification of Standards*, Hayes, Middx: SCAA Publications.

Schwarz, J.C. *et al.* (1974) 'Infant day care: behavioral effects at preschool age', *Developmental Psychology,* 23: 255–61.

Sheridan, M.D. (1969) *The Stycar Sequences,* Windsor: NFER-Nelson.

Sheridan, M.D. (1980) *From Birth to Five Years: Children's Developmental Progress,* 7th edn, Windsor: NFER-Nelson.

Shirley, M.M. (1959) *The First Two Years,* Minnesota: University of Minnesota Press.

Slater, W. (1993) *Dance and Movement in the Primary School: A Cross-curricular Approach to Lesson Planning,* Plymouth: Northcote House Publishers.

Sleap, M. (1988) *Mini Sport,* 2nd edn, London: Heinemann Education Books.

Sleap, M. and Warburton, P. (1992) 'Physical activity levels of 5–11 year old children in England as determined by continuous observation', *Research Quarterly for Exercise and Sport,* 63: 238–45.

Sleap, M. and Warburton, P. (1994) 'Physical activity levels in pre-adolescent children in England', *British Journal of Physical Education Research, Supplement,* 14: 2–6.

Smith, P. K. and Cowie, H. (1991) *Understanding Children's Development,* Oxford: Basil Blackwell.

Smith, R.S. (1982) *Blue-Bell Hill Games,* Harmondsworth: Penguin.

Sports Council (1991) *Everybody Active Project,* Phase 2 Monitoring Report, Strategic Issues 2 Series, London: Sports Council.

Sports Council (1996) 'National junior sports programme', *Sport,* 5: 8–9.

Stafford, I. (1990a) 'Everybody active: Sports Council national demonstration project in England', *Adapted Physical Activity Quarterly,* 6(2).

Stafford, I. (1990b) 'Special school physical education – an attempt to enhance the practice', *British Journal of Physical Education,* 21(2).

Stallings, M.L. (1982) *Motor Learning: From Theory to Practice,* St Louis, Toronto and London: C.V. Mosby Ltd.

Steinberg, L. and Meyer, R. (1995) *Childhood,* London: McGraw Hill.

Steipek, D.J. (1984) 'Young children's performance expectations: logical analysis of wishful thinking', in J.G. Nicols (ed.) *Advances in Motivation and Achievement,* vol. 3, *The Development of Achievement Motivation,* London: JAI Press.

Sugden, D. (1990) 'Development of physical education for all', *British Journal of Physical Education,* 21(1): 247–51.

Sugden, D. (1991) 'The assessment of movement skill problems in 7–9 year old children', *British Journal of Educational Psychology,* 61(3): 329–45.

Sugden, D. and Keogh, J.F. (1990) *Problems in Movement Skill Acquisition,* Columbia: South Carolina Press.

Sugden, D. and Wright, H. (1996) 'Curricular entitlement for all children', in *New Directions in Physical Education,* London: Cassell.

Sutcliffe, M. (1993) *PE Activities,* Bright Ideas for the Early Years Series, Leamington Spa: Scholastic Ltd.

Sutcliffe, M. (1996) 'Looking for quality in children's movements', *Primary PE Focus,* Spring, West Malling, Kent: Physical Education Association of the UK

Tanner, J.M. (1978) *Education and Physical Growth,* London: Hodder & Stoughton.

Titterton, S. (1996) *Dance in Key Stage 2,* BA(Hons) dissertation, University of Durham.

Tizard, B. (1976) 'Effects on play of the child's social class and of the educational orientation of the centre', *Journal of Child Psychology and Psychiatry,* 17: 251–74.

Turner, M. (1989) *Nutrition and Children Aged One to Five,* Fact File 2, London: National Dairy Council.

Turner, M. (1993) *Obesity and Weight Management,* Fact File Number 4, London: National Dairy Council.

Tyler, R.W. (1947) *Basic Principles of Curriculum Instruction*, Chicago and London: University of London Press.

Waan, J.P. and Mon-Williams, M. (1996) 'Clumsiness in children', on-going research, Horsham: Action Research.

Warburton, P. (1995) Editorial, *Primary PE Focus*, Spring, West Malling, Kent: Physical Education Association of the United Kingdom.

Waxman, M. and Stunkard, A. (1980) 'Calorific intake and expenditure of obese boys', *Journal of Paediatrics*, 96: 187–93.

Wetton, P. (1980) 'Interest in large apparatus in nursery school', *Bulletin of Physical Education*, 16(3):1–5.

Wetton, P. (1989a) *Bright Ideas: Games for PE*, Leamington Spa: Scholastic Ltd.

Wetton, P. (1989b) *Physical Education in the Nursery and Infant School*, London: Routledge.

Wetton, P. (1994) 'Physical education as a specialist subject', in C. Aubrey (ed.) *The Role of Subject Knowledge in the Early Years of Schooling*, London: Falmer Press.

Wetton, P. (1996) *Practical Guides: Physical Education: Teaching Within the National Curriculum*, revised edn, Leamington Spa: Scholastic Ltd.

White, A. and Davies, P.S.W. (1994) *National Diet and Nutritional Survey of Children Aged 1 to 4 Years*, London: Department of Health and Social Security.

Williams, A. (ed.) (1989) *Issues in Physical Education for the Primary Years*, London: Falmer Press.

Wiseman, J. (1995) *National Study of Health and Growth in Children Aged 5–11*, London: Department of Health.

Ziegler, E.F. (1977) *Physical Education and Sport Philosophy*, London: Prentice Hall.

Index